MW00748904

"Believe"

An inspirational fable
by Dayle Schear

Blue Dolphin

Published by Blue Dolphin Publishing, Inc.
P.O. Box 8, Nevada City, CA 95959
Orders: 1-800-643-0765
Web: www.bluedolphinpublishing.com

ISBN: 1-57733-084-6

Library of Congress Cataloging-in-Publication Data

Schear, Dayle.
    Believe : an inspirational fable / Dayle Schear.
        p. cm.
    ISBN: 1-57733-084-6
        1. Belief and doubt—Fiction. I. Title.

    PS3569.C476 B4 2000
    813'.54—dc21

                                                    00-040390

Cover design: Dayle Schear

Printed in the United States of America

10   9   8   7   6   5   4   3   2   1

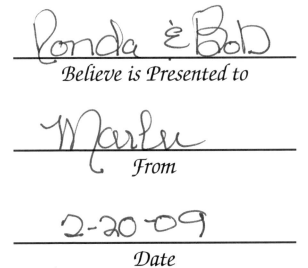

Ronda & Bob

Believe is Presented to

Marlu

From

2-20-09

Date

(For the Homeless)

Introduction

"Believe" is a fable. It's a story of belief and how each character had met with despair . . . Each character had a sordid past and each had lost the passion and motivation to continue his or her life's path. Their Spirit was broken.

Upon finding a book called "Believe," life takes on new meaning for them. For there are several inspirational messages that guide each and every one of the characters, including the reader, into a realm of vision to effect the necessary change's we all need to make in our lives.

What if we could go back in time, change things, right our wrongs. Would we, could we? There is a journey to a realm where our own survival depends on how we handle certain situations in life. Through the power of the book "Believe" it may be possible to change our past.

Ah! the power of belief. Is it real? Is it destiny? Is it a deep desire from within to find answers? If you believe could it mend a broken spirit?

For in all cases our characters find their lives unraveling. There's Joe, once a wealthy handsome man who had it all, only to end up at a homeless camp. Upon reading the book "Believe" he goes back over his life, follows the steps in the book "Believe," makes the necessary changes and turns his life around.

There's Candis, a beautiful young pianist, who gave up her whole career for an abusive, controlling man. After reading "Believe," she's able to take control of her life once again.

The message the book gives you as a reader is that with the power of belief almost anything in life can be changed. If only you "Believe."

PSYCHIC DAYLE SCHEAR

TELEVISION APPEARANCES

Hard Copy Magazine (9 Stories, International Telecast)
Extra (National Telecast)
Sally Jessy Rafael (National Telecast)
Gordon Elliot Show (National Telecast)
Sightings FOX (National Telecast)
Alive & Wellness Show, America's Talking
(National Telecast)
New Year TV Special (FUJI-TV Tokyo, Japan-National)
Hour Magazine CBS (National Telecast)
The Late Show FOX (National Telecast)
AM San Francisco KGO-ABC (Regular 1 Year)
2 At Noon KTVU (Oakland)
ESP & You One Hour Specials
(KGMB-CBS & KITV-ABC, Hawaii, 14 Yrs.)
Your Future One Hour Special (KGMB-CBS Hawaii)
Hawaiian Moving Company (KGMB-CBS Hawaii)
Anchorage Live (KIMO-ABC Alaska)
Good Morning Alaska (KIMO-ABC Alaska)
ESP & You One Hour Special (KIMO-ABC Alaska)
Mystical Healing (Cable 22, Hawaii),
Daytime Show (KOLO-ABC Reno)
KHON News (NBC Hawaii), **KITV News** (ABC Hawaii)
KGMB News (CBS Hawaii), **KOLO News** (ABC Reno),
KHBC (Hilo, Hawaii), **Numerous Telethons** (Charities)

RADIO SHOWS

21st Century Radio (Syndicated Nationally);
KGO, K101, KEST, KALX (San Francisco);
KSSK (K59), KGU, KULA, KKUA, KIKI, KCCN,
I-94, KISA, KMVI, KKON, KPUA, KAUI, KBIG (Hawaii);
KOWL, KTHO, KPTL, KLKT, (Lake Tahoe & Reno);
KENI (Alaska); **WWDB** (Philadelphia); **WCBM** (Baltimore);
KTAR (Arizona); **KTVB** (Texas)

ARTICLES/OTHERS

Washington Times, (Washington DC)
Honolulu Advertiser, Honolulu Star Bulletin
Honolulu Magazine, Honolulu Weekly,
Pets & People, (Hawaii)
Tahoe Tribune, Reno Gazettte,
Nevada Appeal, (Nevada)
The Psychic Reader, (California)
The Spectator, (Massachusetts)
Fate Magazine, (National)

NIGHT CLUBS

Harrah's (Lake Tahoe & Reno, Nevada)
American Hawaii Cruise (Cruise Ship)
Holiday Inn, (Waikiki, Hawaii) **23rd Step** (Hawaii)

Books Published/Others

Dare To Be Different (Autobiography),
The Psychic Within (True Psychic Stories)
Tarot For Beginners (Book & Video),
12-Meditaion Tape Series
Who's Who Of America
Top 100 Psychic Of America (Simon & Schuster)
Aura Awareness (Aura Imaging-Progen)

Acknowledgements

I wish to thank the following people for their encouragement, help and support.

My husband, **Blythe**. A great life teacher. The unknown is your play ground of life. You taught me how to believe. . . .

Peter, my teacher, who has long since passed, but I know he was smiling down on me as I wrote "Believe."

To **Peter Hurkos**, his wife **Stephany** and daughter **Gloria** and her husband **Chris**.

My special thanks to my hanai "calabash" son in Hawaii, **Jeff Rodrigues**. For without his encouragement and picking me up off the floor, every so often, I don't know what I would have done. My son, my love of my life. Thank you so much for always being there for me.

To James Abihai. My close buddy, you are such a wonderful sweetheart. Thanks for your support.

To P.J. and Chance on Maui Thanks for ordering me to finish this book. I love you both. You are two of the kindest people I know; you open your hearts to the world.

To Marcia. Joe, and Bobby Petilleri: Thank you so much for your wonderful inspiration.

Special thanks to my editor, **Maybelle Boyd**. How can I thank you? From the bottom of my heart and the deepest part of my soul you helped me make this book happen. I look upon myself as a learner in this great school of knowledge. Coming from the streets of Newark, New Jersey I had very little schooling, flunking English and being dyslexic to boot. Yet, you helped me gather my thoughts, put everything in its proper place and taught me the value of writing.

This book "Believe" was special, for it gave me hope to Believe once again. This is my fourth book. And I hope to God, Maybelle, you never give up on me, for somewhere in time we'll have a winner. All we have to do is "Believe."

Thank you. . . .

Special thanks to **Karin Beals**, my wonderful partner in crime. You see, Karin is a writer as well. There are many times we sit in my writing room just exchanging ideas. I never get writer's block, because all I have to do is buff an idea over to Karin. She takes the ball to the finish line and a story is written.

But what Karin doesn't know is, the Idea Fairy is visiting her and giving me this very special information that's in her head. We are writing partners in life. In fact, she was working so hard on her new trade of photography, she just didn't have time to be here all the time to help me finish this book.

But there will be many other books we can share and many of her photos will appear in my upcoming books. So hurry, Karin, and finish your photo classes, for there is a need for you to write by my side. Thank you again for being you.

Special thanks to **Grandma Fern** In Heaven With your passing in 1999, I have felt your spiritual presence. I have felt your light and love with the will to go on. In life you were so special. I know now God is watching over you.

Belief Is In The Spirit Of Your Heart

"Believe"

If you "Believe . . ." Your journey will begin!

Chapter 1

"Believe"

An inspirational fable

By Dayle Schear

The story I am about to tell you takes place in New York City. If I hadn't experienced it myself, I would have believed this to be a wondrous tale. You see, I'm a writer; I get my material from ordinary people like you.

It wasn't long after my father's death when I seemed to drop out of society. Life didn't have much meaning for me any more, for he had been the love of my life.

He was a workaholic, quite a businessman and a wheeler dealer all his life. He didn't have a lot of time for me nor, for that matter, anyone else. But the time we did spend together was wonderful. He taught me all about life. He taught me how to live. He taught me how to help mankind.

I was at my father's side when he died. He was quite spiritual upon his passing. While lying on his death bed, he motioned for me to move closer to him. As he took his last breath, he whispered in my ear. The words he whispered changed my life forever. My father always taught me "If you believe, many wondrous things can happen."

Ah! the power of belief. Is it a myth? Is it a grand adventure? Is it direct information that guides each and every one of us to our destiny?

For the tale I tell you is pure of heart. It has meaning; it has purpose. It will change your life, I promise. If you follow along carefully you will hear the very words my father whispered in my ear on the day of his passing. Words that have changed my life forever. Soon those very words will change your life as well! So, as this tale was told to me, I will pass it on to you.

My story starts off in the city of New York on a very dark, frightfully cold evening, snow falling gently through the air.

Three homeless people huddled around a burning garbage can, rubbing their hands together to keep warm.

Joe, one of the homeless men, eyed a brown NYC refuse dumpster off in the distance. He broke away from the group momentarily, all eyes following him. His gloves exposed his raw red fingers to the harsh cold as he rummaged through the garbage.

Ah! An epicurean delight is found. Joe mumbled and grumbled under his breath while tearing the paper off a half-eaten hot dog. He devoured the remnants.

While reaching in the dumpster for more food, he

found a book. The gold lettering on the cover caught his eye. He read out loud one simple word, "Believe."

"Believe!"

Intrigued by this word "Believe" he began thumbing through the pages. The first sentence astounded him.

"It's time to forgive yourself." He read on. "If you follow the steps in this book, your whole life will change. This book is special; this book is for you; this book will change your life, if you Believe."

Joe sat down on the cold pavement, engrossed in the book.

1. Look back over your life and figure out what caused you to take this path you're on.

2. Try with all your heart to go back in time, if possible, and make amends with the situation that put you in this position.

3. Now change the outcome of this situation; if possible, physically or within your own mind.

4. Believe that you can change your life. Believe that it was you who created your life to be the way it is now. Believe your life can change only if you really want it to. Believe! For all things are possible when we believe.

5. *If you follow these steps your whole life will change.*

6. *Some of the rewards of these steps are you will be able to forgive yourself and others, love will surely find you, and you will find your own destiny.*

7. *However, after the change has begun, you must pass the book and knowledge on to someone in need, or all will be taken away from you. Let the light shine in. Let the journey begin.*

A tear rolled down Joe's cheek. As he threw his head into his hands, he remembered his sordid past.

Once a stock broker on Wall Street in the early eighties, Joe had plenty of money. He was flourishing. He had everything to live for and always lived his life in the fast lane. Money to burn. Tall, dark and handsome, he had a girl on every corner. Joe had it all and used it to his advantage.

Joe had come from a broken home. His father Paul, who drank himself into a stupor daily, left the family one day, never to return. His mother was a weak, timid woman who had allowed her husband to control and abuse her at will, physically, emotionally, and mentally. By the time he left, she was numb.

Joe took on the task of raising his two brothers and a sister. He worked at two jobs and went to school at night.

He was determined never to be poor like his father and never to abandon his family, never to marry. Joe wanted it all. "Poor no more" was his motto.

As the years passed, with the huge amount of money he made in the stock market, he was able to buy a house for cash for his mom. He was king. Buying and selling was his lot. He thought he had it all . . . until he met Mary.

While walking down the hall to his office one Friday, Joe saw Mary bending over, picking up some papers she dropped on the floor. Joe paused. Mary was a petite blonde with blue eyes that sparkled when she looked up at him. He smiled with that charismatic smile of his and helped Mary gather her paperwork from the floor.

"Hi, my name is Joe. You must be new around here. What's your name?" he asked.

"Mary. Yes, I'm new. I work down the hall for Mr. Prescott; I'm his new secretary. Thank you so much for helping me, Joe. Well, nice to have met you. I guess I better go." She smiled.

Their eyes locked. It was as if she knew Joe. There was something very familiar about him. Mary turned and walked toward the office.

"Hey, Mary!" Joe shouted. "Can we have lunch tomorrow? Maybe I can show you around and have you meet some of the co-workers so you won't feel so awkward around here."

"Sure, that would be nice. My extension is 240. Give me a ring when you're ready." She smiled again.

Joe was feeling cocky now, self assured. Just another conquest, he thought. "Whoa! I can't wait to get my hands on this one," he mumbled softly under his breath.

The next day Mary and Joe met downstairs at an outside cafe. They were getting to know each another. Mary was in her late twenties and had a secretarial degree from one of the finest business schools in New York. She was studying to be a stockbroker.

Mary and Joe hit it off. He was fascinated by her. Every evening he would teach Mary about stocks and give her fine pointers into the stock market. She ate it up like candy. As the months passed, they were bonding closer and closer. For the first time in his life Joe felt alive.

There was something special about Mary; she wasn't like all the rest of his bimbo babes. Mary was not only intelligent, but also so soft and demure. Joe found Mary to be very spiritual and romantic. She was loving, tender, and kind.

As the months rolled by he was beginning to fall in love with her. There were picnics in the park and wonderful candlelight dinners. Making love to Mary was not mechanical like all the rest; it was more of an art.

Mary was quite taken by Joe. Although she knew he was a playboy, she was enjoying the attention and the ride.

One evening Mary looked into Joe's eyes and asked. "Do you believe in soul-mates?"

"Soul-mates. What does that mean?" he asked.

"Well, Joe, it's when two people meet, two people like you and me, who are very comfortable with each other. It's as if we knew each other before somewhere in time. We complement each other. At times we're one. A soul- mate is the missing part of you," she explained.

Joe shook his head in confusion. "Mary, I don't know about soul-mates. I just know I have very deep feelings for you. I believe in my work; I believe in making money. I believe in working hard. Soul-mates I don't know."

"But Joe, we've been together for only a few months and you finish my sentences. You even know what I want for breakfast before I do. Doesn't that tell you some-thing?" She cocked her head, waiting for an answer.

"Yes, my Dolling. . . . It tells me I'm deeply enticed by you and want you more and more every day. That's what it tells me." Joe chuckled.

"Oh, Joe, I guess you don't get it!"

Joe, could sense that Mary was frustrated. "Okay, tell me more." He then gave Mary his undivided attention.

"Joe, I really believe in this stuff. I've been reading some books and we seem to fit what they're saying. You see, there is a theory about soul-mates versus twin-souls. Every person on earth has a twin or twin-soul. The theory goes when God created man there lay his other half. It created a longing so deep within us that we knew some part of us was missing." Mary looked up to make sure Joe was paying attention. He seemed fascinated.

She continued. "Lifetime after lifetime we search for each other. We grow and go our separate ways, each of us learning to grow in our own perfect way without each other, before we can complete each other. We search for our other half on earth or in the heavens, a search that can become desperate and filled with wrong relationships, times of sadness, times of sorrow, till our twin arrives so we can become one with the universe."

Joe interrupted. "So that's why I've had so many weird relationships. You mean it's because I never found the right one?"

"Yes, Joe, now you're getting it. Let me continue," she said.

Joe nodded.

"Joe, look at me; look in my eyes." Her tone was demanding. "Joe, there is only one twin-soul lifetime after lifetime. For without the reuniting of this one soul we will feel an emptiness inside of us."

"Mary, what's the difference between a soul-mate and a twin-soul?" Joe asked.

"We have many soul-mates . . . friends, lovers, and bosses. It means when two souls mate we become one for a short period in time. We learn all our lessons from that person, then we can stay around or move on. The choice is up to us.

"But a twin-soul . . . there is but one in the whole universe. We were born to be together. That is our twin-soul. Only one, Joe, only one." Mary stared deeply into Joe's eyes.

Joe grabbed Mary and kissed her. They made love all night long.

The next morning she asked, "Well, Joe, what do you think?"

"Only time will tell, Mary." He smiled.

Well, time did tell. Months swiftly turned into their one-year anniversary. Joe was more in love with Mary than ever. He couldn't sleep for the want to be with her. His work was beginning to be affected. He had to be with her, he had to have her.

But Joe had a major conflict: he didn't believe in marriage. He was both mother and father to his brothers and sister. He made a promise to himself he would never marry, but Joe never counted on falling in love with Mary. He wanted to live with her, but marriage was out of the question.

Mary, on the other hand, was very traditional. She believed in marriage. She wanted a family. She wanted to grow old with Joe and within her heart and soul she knew Joe was her twin-Soul.

Mary wasn't feeling well lately; she decided to go to

the doctor to see what was wrong. The doctor called her at home to let her know the results of her blood test. She was pregnant. Mary didn't expect this; she and Joe had always used protection. The test must be wrong. She asked the doctor if she could take another test. Positive once more. She was confused.

She wanted to keep this baby. She didn't believe in abortion and she was sure Joe would be happy. He didn't have to marry her right away, she thought. "A child of our own. I know Joe will be happy; he loves me so much. I'll tell him tonight over dinner."

Mary waited for Joe at their usual private table at Sardi's. When he walked in, she noticed how handsome he was, dressed in a well-fitted gray suit, tie undone and top button loose on his shirt.

Joe couldn't wait to relax with a drink and Mary. He bent over and gave her a kiss on her cheek.

"Hey, Babe, how was your day?"

"Really good, Joe," she replied.

"Ready to order, Babe?"

"Yes." Mary moved closer to Joe, almost snuggling. She would tell him the news after dinner.

The last course was served. Mary was starting to feel secure in her thoughts.

"Joe, something happened today."

Joe looked into Mary's eyes; he knew she was serious.

"Tell me what's bothering you. Come on, I can handle it."

Mary hesitated for a second, then blurted out, "I'm pregnant." She hung her head down.

What came next was totally unexpected.

"Pregnant! What!" He jumped up from the table. "Waiter! Check, I want the check now!" he shouted.

Mary tried to calm him. "Joe, sit down; let's discuss this."

"There's nothing to discuss. I can't handle this right now in my life. Mary, I love you so much, I just want it to be you and me. Don't you understand? I don't want kids. I raised my whole family. It's my turn now."

Heads began to turn toward their table.

"Joe, this was unforeseen, but there are no accidents. You know I believe this baby is meant to be. I want this baby. I don't believe in abortion. Besides, this is our child," she pleaded.

Joe was unmoved. He drove Mary home in silence. When finally he spoke his voice had an edge to it.

"I have nothing to say to you, Mary. You know how I feel. Women, when they want to trap a man, they get pregnant. Well, it just won't work. Do you understand? It won't work."

Joe let Mary out of the car and muttered, "Later." He drove off in a huff.

Back in her apartment, Mary cried all night long.

Days turned into agonizing weeks. Joe passed Mary in the hall at work on several occasions. He refused to look at her, refused to talk to her. There was nothing she could do.

Mary was devastated, but she was strong in her beliefs. She was going to keep the baby. Every evening she hoped and prayed Joe would call. Not a word.

The weeks turned into months, yet no word from Joe. He was determined to put Mary out of his mind.

Joe was so distraught he telephoned his two brothers and sister and called for a meeting. Arriving in Long Island late that evening, he sat for hours explaining his situation.

His brothers Tony and Mario didn't have a whole lot to say. They seemed disappointed in their brother. They expected much more from him. They let their sister Jan do the talking.

Jan was furious with Joe for she knew what a womanizer he truly was.

"Joe, when are you going to grow up? You have it all. You say you love this girl—well, why don't you marry her? You know it's the right thing to do."

Joe was clearly agitated by her remarks. "Jan, I just can't do it. I won't be roped into anything. She just got pregnant so I would marry her. Well, I'm not ready for marriage! Do you understand?"

"Joe, I wash my hands of you. Who's going to take care of that girl and her child? How can you just leave her? You know, I thought I knew my brother, but I don't know you anymore. If you don't help her in some way, I don't want to have anything to do with you!" Jan shouted. "I'm sure I speak for Tony and Mario."

Jan turned to her brothers sitting quietly on the couch. They nodded. They knew this subject drove Jan crazy; they weren't about to interfere.

Joe was angry. "Well, if that's the way you want it, I have only one thing to say to all of you—I don't have a family anymore!" Joe slammed the door and drove off.

Then the unforeseen event occurred, the stock market crashed. All of Joe's investments went south. There was nothing left. Pandemonium set in within his office. He spent many nights at the local bar, drinking his way to oblivion. Everything he had worked so hard for now fell by the wayside. Joe drank away his troubles from morning to night. There went his job. Finally, the local bartender couldn't extend any more credit to Joe.

Meanwhile, Mary was lying in the hospital, giving birth to their son Michael. All alone with not a soul in the world to help her, Mary was so brave as Michael made his way screaming and crying into this world.

As for Joe, well, he found himself on the streets of New York with the homeless. That's where he lived this life for well over a year.

So this is where our story began.

Joe tossed and turned in his sleep. Flashes of Mary's face flooded his dreams, while he relived all the things he had been running away from. When he awoke, Joe realized this night of hell would be his last night on the streets. The noises of the night intensified and terrified him for the first time.

He clutched his book "Believe" and opened it to the words he felt deep within his soul.

"Believe"

Every person has the power to take control of his life; it's never too late to change; it's never too late to improve and make your life better.

You must accept whatever will come your way, for the power of change is within your very grasp.

Don't be afraid to admit that you are less than perfect; let those you love help you. Always believe in miracles!

Joe held the book so very tightly to his chest. He knew now what he had to do. He brushed himself off and made his way to the YMCA. Joe had now made his decision to clean up his life and to right his wrong with Mary.

At the YMCA he showered, shaved and borrowed some clothes. Feeling better, he walked the streets of New York City looking for work. He saw a help-wanted sign at the New Rage Deli. He walked in the door and asked to speak to the manager.

"Hi my name is Joe. I see you need some help here," he said with that charismatic smile. "I believe I'm the man for the job."

"My name is Al. I'm the owner. What's your work history?"

Joe proceeded to tell him.

Al wiped his hands on the apron tied around his waist. "Well, it's only a dish-washing job, but if you want, I'll give you a shot. Oh, by the way, Joe, you get two free meals a day here and all the coffee you can drink."

"I'll take it. When can I start?"

Al smiled. "Here's my apron, Pal."

Joe worked all day, happy to have a job for the first time in a long while. He took a room in the back of the deli for a short period of time and worked long and hard till he was able to save a little. Several weeks later his confidence was building; he had a little money in his pocket.

Every night he would open his book "Believe" and read a little while slowly falling asleep. The book seemed to comfort him.

"Believe"

While going through life, the best way is to take it slowly; its the simplest way to get ahead.

One step at a time. Don't look back, for if you do you'll never see what lies ahead.

*By the time you reach the top of the hill, you will
have become better and a stronger person, stronger than
you ever were before.*

*One step at a time. One moment at a time. One day at
a time. Follow your dreams and watch them come true.
All you have to do is "Believe."*

One Sunday morning Joe decided this was the day he
would search for Mary and his child. He found a phone
booth and feverishly began looking up Mary's phone
number. Finding her number as well as her address, he
deposited fifty cents and slowly dialed Mary's number. He
listened in silence as Mary answered with a sweet voice,
then, shaking his head, he hung up the phone quietly. He
put Mary's address in the back pocket of his jeans.

Walking, walking, walking, Joe arrived at Third Avenue. He paused when he reached the apartment building
at 748 Third Avenue. Joe checked the directory. "There
she is, Mary James; that's her." He took a deep breath.
"This is it." Joe climbed up several flights of stairs and
almost was out of breath when he reached the apartment.
He paused to catch his breath. He stared intensely at the
door. Then, he knocked.

Mary checked the peephole to see who was knocking.
She gasped when she recognized Joe. She was overcome
with emotion. For the first few months after their breakup,

Mary had sat by the phone, waiting for Joe to call. He never did.

She had thought about him day and night from the time she woke up in the morning till the time she went to sleep. She believed with all her heart and soul that some day Joe would return, and now that day had come. It was the moment she has been waiting for all these months.

Mary quickly unlocked the door. She stared at Joe and, after a pause, passionately embraced him. They held each other so tightly; no words needed to be said.

Mary gently reached out for Joe's hand and led him to the bedroom to see his son for the first time. Joe dropped to his knees as Michael turned and looked at him for the first time.

Mary said softly, "This is your dad."

They embraced once more as Joe cried and told Michael and Mary how sorry he was for leaving them. He begged them to give him one more chance.

Mary nodded. They would pick up the pieces of their once-tattered life together.

Time passed. Mary and Joe were getting to know each other quite well. She still worked at the stock exchange, well on her way to becoming a stockbroker. Michael was now approaching his second birthday. Joe had now become the father of the year; he did everything with his son for his son.

Joe decided to get into computers; he didn't want to go back into the world of gambling and stocks. He wanted his life to be simple.

Joe remembered what he read the other night in the book "Believe."

"*Believe*"

Before I leave this world I want my child to know a few very important things about who I am and what I believe.

I know in my heart it may not make a big difference in the grand scheme of things, but in my heart I feel I will have shared my truths of my soul.

I want my child to know about spirit. I want him to know that the world is not all about money. I want him to know it's about love and sharing from the deepest soul of his heart.

That I love him, with all that I am; and wherever his journey in life leads him I will be with him in spirit as well as soul. He will always have my love wherever he goes.

Joe told Mary all about the book "Believe" and how he found it in the dumpster. He finally understood what she meant by soul-mates, for there hadn't been a waking moment while he was among the homeless that he didn't pine for the loss of her. He needed courage to find his way back home to Mary.

Mary was so happy. Their life together was like a story book; things were falling into place. The love of their life was their son Michael. Every weekend Joe and Mary and Michael played at the park. There would be many long picnics. Soon they would be married.

On one of their Sunday picnics they noticed Michael seemed to have difficulty breathing. Suddenly, Michael turned a bluish purple. Mary screamed for Joe as he sat on the bench reading his book "Believe."

"Joe! Come here quickly!"

Joe raced to Mary, who held Michael in her arms.

"Lets get him to the hospital. I think he stopped breathing." Joe tried to remain calm while breathing into Michael's lungs until help could arrive.

Mary called 911 on her cellular phone. Within minutes the ambulance arrived and the paramedics somehow got Michael breathing again. Sirens blaring, they rushed him to the hospital.

Joe paced the halls of the hospital while Mary stood by her son's side.

"Why is this happening to me?" Joe cried, his eyes filled with tears. "He's so young and helpless. Oh, dear God, what can I do to make him better? Please, God, give me a sign. Please, God, save my son. I'm begging you."

The book "Believe" fell out of his pants pocket onto the floor. Was it a sign? Joe picked up the book and read:

"Believe"

Never give up. Never let go of your dreams and never let go of the love you have inside of you. One day your life will come together; What you have wished for has finally come to be. One day you will look back on this moment in time and ask yourself, "How did I get through all that?"

Why, of course, the answer is Because You Believed.

Joe looked up from the book and closed his eyes for a moment. He remembered Step 7: After the change has begun, you must pass the book and knowledge to someone in need, or all will be taken away from you. Let the light shine in. Let the journey begin.

"I'll have to pass on this book . . . that's one of the rules in the book. If I don't pass on this book to the next person, my life will revert back to the way it was. That's it! I know that's it.

"I have to get out of this hospital and go back to the homeless. I have to pass the book on."

Joe ran into the room where Mary was holding Michael's hand.

"Mary, trust me . . . I'll be right back. Just trust me," he said hurriedly

Mary nodded.

Joe ran as fast as he could to the park where he knew he could find the homeless. Hardly anyone recognized him. Joe passed by a shadow of a man perched on a box against an old doorway The man was wearing a torn and tattered gray sweat suit. His beard and mustache were stringy and caked with remnants of food.

Shocked by what he saw, Joe stopped abruptly at the doorway. Joe shouted. "Nick! Nick, it's me, Joe, remember?"

Nick stopped drinking from his wine bottle and peered up at Joe. "Joe it's you! It's really you, isn't it? Whoa, what happened you come into some money, Pal? Can I have a hit on a cigarette? Got some spare change?"

Joe interrupted Nick's rambling. "Nick buddy, listen to me! You got to listen to me. I don't have much time; please listen." Joe sat down beside Nick on the cold concrete slab.

Nick glared at Joe's red face and took another swig from his bottle. "Yeah, I'm listening. Give me a cigarette and I'll listen all you want, Buddy."

Joe found an old cigarette butt in the gutter and lit it for Nick.

"Nick, I have a book to give you. Please read it. This book changed my life. "Here, Nick, please . . . take the book."

"What is this book?" Nick thumbed through the pages randomly. "Com'on, Joe, how can anyone believe a book can change his life? This must be hogwash. Nothing can change my life," Nick muttered.

"Nick, look at me." Joe shook the book in front of Nick's face. "This book gave me back my life. Look at me, Nick. Trust someone for once in your life," Joe pleaded. "Read the book. That's all I ask."

"Nick, I have to go." Joe stared at Nick's face, silently pleading with Nick. This was Joe's mission; he had to give back to the homeless.

He turned and walked away, hoping with all his heart and soul that Nick would read this very precious book.

Joe raced back towards the hospital, thinking, "If I'm right, my son should be getting better. I gave the book away to someone in need. I fulfilled my mission."

When Joe reached the hospital floor, he was out of breath. There was Mary holding her son in her arms. She smiled at Joe and just nodded. "He's going to make it," said Mary.

"I know, Mary. I've been praying. We're all going to make it." He looked into Mary's eyes and said, "All we had to do was 'Believe!'"

"Believe"

For to find love, look in the heart of your spirit.

Chapter 2

"Believe"

Nick fittled as he opened the book and reads ever so slowly:

"Believe"

1. Believe! Only you hold the power to believe. All things are possible when you believe. You may be at your lowest point in your life now, but soon all things will change if you believe.

2. There is hope. You are not alone. Face your fears; it's time to undo the wrong in your life. You have punished yourself long enough. You can fix the past.

3. You can grow within from your emotional pain. You can learn your lessons from the past. Know the pain you face today will only last for a short while. Your life is changing right now as you read this book.

4. There is no comfort in self pity. It's time for you to change your course of action, even though it is said,

"Don't change horses in midstream." When your horse dies, you change horses.

5. It's time to take a good look at your life and see where you went wrong. It's time to take control. For all is possible if you right that wrong and believe.

Nick paused as he read those words; they somehow startled him. He looked up at the stars in the vast heavens as he wondered whether he could change his life. Was it possible? Why, all he had to do was believe. Was it really that simple?

Nick clutched the book to his chest and slowly drifted off to sleep for the very first time in years. A feeling of peace and contentment came over him. While Nick slept, flashes of moments past rapidly flashed through his mind. He saw all the pain he caused others.

He was once a young thriving attorney in the city of New York. Standing a wiry six feet tall and sporting a well-groomed mustache, Nick was charismatic to the max. Woman fell to their feet when they saw him. Nick was then at the top of his firm. His downfall was his love of money, sex, and power.

Nick lived his life to the fullest. He wined and dined anyone and everyone. He took chances with other people's money. He was always looking for the pie in the sky. Nick thought he could turn sixty thousand dollars into six million with his get-rich-quick schemes.

There wasn't enough power to feed his ego; he always wanted more. For more than a period of five years he relied on his good looks to swindle a number of women from their hard-earned money. He charmed both men and women to invest their life savings in wild adventures. Nick had the gift of gab.

But his past soon caught up with him. It was only a matter of time before Nick's friends wised up and demanded their money back. Nick dug his hole deeper and deeper. Now he had to borrow money from other people to pay his friends.

Nick had not always been this way. It took him four tries to pass the state bar and he struggled night and day to make it as an attorney. He came from a poor family in upstate New York, so Nick had to finance his dream of becoming an attorney by himself.

He had no time for a wife; He was only thirty-five and was determined to be a successful attorney. To Nick, woman were used as trophies, toys for him. Each beautiful lady he dated would bring him one step closer to achieving his life's goals: Money! Sex! Freedom! Power! That's what he lived for. He worked endlessly eighteen hours a day to network and achieve these goals.

Now, mind you, he wasn't a bad attorney. But being the

young Italian stud that he was, he stole from the rich on occasion.

Nick would always find a deal, a new investment, that invariably would fail. His deals started off well, but as time passed his $50,000 deal would falter. There would go all the money that he had invested.

He was in a jam this time. Several people were demanding there money back.

Along came Nancy, a beautiful young blonde model. One look into Nick's eyes and she was hopelessly in love. When Nick learned that Nancy had managed to save $30,000 over the years while modeling, he moved in for the kill.

He had to pay back one of his investors rather quickly, so he devised a scheme for Nancy consisting of a high interest loan. He promised her within six months he could give her twenty percent on her money. Nancy was hooked. With Nancy's $30,000 check, Nick paid back with interest the investor who had been hounding him. She was pleased.

Nick's method of operation was as follows: Six months later he would go back to the same investors and borrow the money again, promising them he would pay them back within six months at a higher interest rate.

The scheme went on and on till he was in so deep in debt that he had to borrow money from the Mob.

Now the Mob is not a real good place to borrow money from. They don't take kindly to not being paid back. But Nick would offer his services as an attorney to the Mob; if they needed a favor, Nick would have to perform.

On one occasion one of the mob bosses had to rough up one of his local venders who had not paid up. Nick was called in that night to video-tape the hit. While the cameras were rolling, a murder took place. The Mob wanted it's money and the poor guy couldn't pay. The tape was necessary to show the boss that everything had been taken care of. Of course, Nick witnessed the incident. He was told to keep the tape in his office safe. If anyone found out, Nick would be killed as well. Nick locked the video-tape up securely, figuring his debt was being paid to the Mob.

But within months Nick's friends were hounding him to pay on their investments. One deal after the next was faltering by the wayside. He was in well over his head. He even got to the point where he put up his office furniture as collateral to each person to whom he owed money.

Now the grandest scheme was yet to be played.

Nick's next mark was an old friend named Susan. Nick grew up with Susan in New York. Whenever she was in trouble, Nick was always there to help her.

This was one of those rare times. Susan found herself in small claims court one day suing a book distributor. You see, she just released her new self-published book when

John, her distributor, decided to declare bankruptcy. He kept all her books and all her hard-earned money from their world-wide sales.

Susan had sunk every dime that she had into her book. She couldn't afford an attorney and had too much pride to ask her father for help. So she showed up in court alone, not knowing what to do.

Nick happened to be in the same courtroom that day, defending one of his clients, when he noticed Susan sitting there alone. During a courtroom break he went over to her.

"Hey Sue, what are you doing here?"

Susan was happy to see her old friend. "Hi, Nick. I'm suing John for stealing my money and my books," she said.

Nick asked, "Do you have an attorney?"

"No, can't afford one."

Nick said, "Susan, let me help you."

She nodded and filled Nick in so he could approach the bench. The judge allowed Nick to be her attorney and gave them a different court date so Nick could be briefed by his client.

Nick promised to defend her at no charge. Nick went to court for Susan, but, unfortunately, John was really bankrupt and there was no money. Nick and Susan remained very good friends.

Several weeks passed when Nick rang up Susan just to chat. "Hey, Sue, what's up?"

Susan cried, "Nick, what's wrong? I can hear it in your voice. Something's wrong!"

Nick sighed. "Well, I have a case that's called a binding arbitration. That means I've already won the case, but they want me to put up a 100,000 dollar bond. I don't have the money."

Susan, feeling bad for Nick, said, "Maybe I can help? Let me check around a bit. I'll call you back in a few hours."

Susan called her father and explained how Nick had helped her over the years. She told her dad that Nick now needed help. Her father said he could take out a $50,000 home equity loan, provided that Nick make the monthly payments.

"Great, Dad! I'll tell him and call you back?"

Susan told Nick what her father had offered. Nick was elated.

"Look, Susan, this arbitration will be over in sixty days. You tell your dad I'll do more than make the payments. I'll even give him twenty percent on his money, I promise." Nick was dead serious.

The deal was done. Nick borrowed the other $50,000 from another friend to whom he gave the same story . . . that he could make a twenty-percent gain within sixty days.

Over the months Nick was really good about paying the

home equity loan on Susan's father's house but It wasn't long before Nick ran into money problems again. He couldn't make the loan payment that month and didn't know what to say to Susan.

Susan, meanwhile, always stayed on top of things. She checked with the bank every month to ensure the loan payments were made. But that month was different: no payment. Susan went into a rage. She drove to Nick's office and barged in, screaming at him.

"Nick, what is going on? You promised to make the payments on my father's loan. Are you out of your mind? I trusted you. What kind of trouble are you in?"

Seeing how furious Susan was, Nick had to come up with a story. "Susan, I can't lie to you. I'm in trouble. The judge extended the binding arbitration and I don't know when I'll get the money back. I'm up to my ears in bills and I'm one step a way from locking the doors on this office. I promise you I will find away to get the money to pay your dad's loan. I promise."

Susan sat down beside Nick and stared into his eyes. "Nick, I trusted you. You are my friend. I believed in you. If you don't get that money, my father could lose his house. I don't have any money to pay the house payments. Please, I'm begging you . . . find a way to make good on your promise."

For the first time in years Nick felt ashamed. He bowed

his head down. He had a special bond with Susan; she was like a sister to him. She was the last person in the world he wanted to hurt.

"Susan, I will! If I have to steal the money, I will, Darling," he assured her. Com'on, let's grab a bite to eat; we can talk." Nick and Susan went downstairs to a small coffee shop to finish their conversation.

"Nick, it's all over town that you're in trouble. What is going on?" she asked.

"I made a few bad deals, that's all. I'm trying like hell to make good on them but no one will give me the time of day."

During their lunch, Nick received a phone call on his cellular phone. He nodded and said, "Yes, of course," several times. When the conversation was over he looked at Susan and said, "I shouldn't tell you this, but that was a call from a friend. I'm hiding his video tape in my office safe for him. If anyone finds out, I could be dead."

Susan was shaken. "Nick, what have you got yourself into? Is it drugs? Drinking? Loan sharking? What is it?"

"None of the above. I don't do drugs, you know that. I just made a few bad deals and now it's catching up with me. That's all, I swear." Nick shrugged.

Susan sensed there was more to the story, but she kept her suspicions to her- self. "Okay, we'll find away to get me this month's payment for my dad's house loan. And

Nick, I really don't care where you get it from. I don't care who you steal it from, as long as I get that payment." Susan's voice was escalating louder with each sentence.

"Done! Come to my office tomorrow; I'll have the money for you."

The next day, Nick had the payment for her. Susan was relieved. Months were passing. Nick always had the payment, but not without Susan's screaming and yelling at him to get it. Their relationship was straining.

She never knew if Nick would pay back the money or not. She held her breath every month. The stress took a toll on her health.

Rumors were spreading all over town about Nick. There was even talk of the Mob putting out a contract on him. He had borrowed so much money from so many that there was little or no hope for him.

Every day Susan heard a different story about Nick. Women seemed to be his easiest mark. He would use his charm, she heard, to swindle them out of their money so he could pay some of his other people. Susan decided to check into things further. This became an obsession with her to get back her father's money.

The further she checked, the more ludicrous the stories became. It was time for her to confront Nick.

When Susan walked into Nick's office unannounced, she was in for a surprise. There was the sheriff ready to serve Nick with papers of some sort. Clients taking his furniture out of his office, the Mob ready to hit this poor fellow, now the sheriff! What was going on?

Nick pulled Susan over to the side and whispered in her ear, "Susan, back me up here. Help as much as you can." Nick's hands were shaking. He was being evicted from his office for non-payment of rent.

Susan approached the officer. "Sheriff, can you give us a few hours?" she pleaded. "Maybe I can straighten out this mess.

The sheriff was not moved He replied, "Lady, why should I give this shyster any time at all? Why, he swindled half the town out of their money."

Susan pleaded some more. "Good point, Officer, but look at the mess we have here. If you arrest Nick, no one will get their money back. Don't you understand? If he declares bankruptcy, everyone loses. Give me some time with him, just a few hours. Then if you want to lock up the place, it's up to you." Chaos was mounting everyone talking at once. "Let's achieve some calm in this office, please," the sheriff said.

Somehow it worked. The sheriff cleared everyone out of the office so Susan could talk to Nick.

"Nick, sit down. Drink some water," she said, handing him a glass.

Nick held his head in his shaking hands. "Susan, help me. What can I do?"

"Nick, let's clear out some important things. Go get whatever is important in your office," she said. "What about that video tape you told me about at lunch last week? Shouldn't you be getting that out of your safe?"

Nick leaped out from his chair. "My god, the tape! I can't believe you remembered that." He quickly retrieved the tape from his safe and packed everything he could in a few boxes.

Susan helped him carry his life's worth of papers out to the car. What Susan didn't know was she had just saved Nick's life. The video tape belonged to the Mob. Nick now owed her his life, for if the sheriff had got hold of that tape he would have had evidence to put Nick and his friends away for life. Without knowing it, Susan was a life saver. What a day.

Within weeks it was all over the papers that Nick was disbarred. He was no longer an attorney. Susan knew she had to find away to get the $50,000 back at all costs.

Thinking, thinking, thinking . . . Susan wracked her brain till there was nothing left to think about. She nearly went mad. She started backtracking on Nick. She was determined to interview every person who knew him; she had to find his vice. Weeks went by; this wasn't getting any easier. Finally, there was a break.

Susan received a phone call that afternoon from a girl named Rose, a stripper from the East Side.

Rose said, "Hello, Susan, you don't know me, but I

think I have some important and useful information about Nick for you. Can you meet me at The Cafe on 4th street in about an hour?"

"Yes, I'm on my way!" Susan shouted as she hung up her phone. Susan ran out her front door and hailed a cab.

"The Cafe on 4th street. And hurry!

Sitting in The Cafe, Susan realized she had no idea who she was waiting for. Suddenly, a young lady appeared out of nowhere and sat down next to her.

"Hi, I'm Rose. Just listen to me for a moment," she said softly. Rose inched her way close to Susan. "Look, it's all over town about Nick. We girls that work at the club know all about him. What I'm about to tell you can't be repeated. You could put our lives in danger. Do you understand?"

Susan nodded.

"Nick has been hanging around our club for about five years. He dates several of our girls but what you don't know is he pays a very high price to hang out with us. I know this will sound strange but some of the girls charge 1,000 dollars per hour."

Susan gasped.

"Yes, it's true. We figure he has spent several hundred thousand dollars just dating us, if you know what I mean. Susan, you're too nice to hang around someone like him. He's a degenerate. He loves his women; he's addicted, and he will pay any price to be with one of us." Rose stared directly into Susan's eyes, which were filled with tears.

"Oh my god! How can I get my father's money back! Nick spent every dime on women. I mean, are you sure he doesn't gamble? I know he doesn't drink or do drugs . . . but women? How can anyone spend that amount of money over the years?" She turned to Rose. "No offense. I mean, I just don't get it." Tears flowed down her cheeks.

"Sorry, Honey. He's a sucker. Most men are, you know. If given the chance, they all would spend a night with one of us girls. Nick's no different. He's a love addict; there isn't enough love or sex in the world for him. Do you get it?"

"Yes." Susan more than got it. "How can I get my money back?"

"Well, Honey, there is only one way . . . con the con. He'll bite. I gotta go. And Susan, we never had this conversation." Rose got up from the table and exited.

Susan was in shock. How could Nick, her friend, do this to her and all the other women he swindled! Susan was determined to get her money back. She sat for days thinking up ways to con Nick. Finally, she thought of an elaborate plan. Women were his vice; he needed money to pay for women, so he swindled everyone out of their money. Well, now it was time for Nick to get swindled.

Susan had a lot of friends, especially on the lower east side of town. She remembered how the Mob owed her a favor for saving the video tape. So she decided it was time to ask for help from Big Al, who owned a high-class strip joint in town and who she knew had connections with the Mob. She explained the long drawn out story in detail to Big Al. After listening intensely to Susan, he, of course, thought it would be easier to just bump Nick off, but that wasn't the answer. Susan explained why she needed the $50,000 back, and if Nick were dead she would never get her money back. Al saw her point, and Al agreed to help her.

To make a long story short, after weeks of planning and planning, Al invited Nick to the Club Mex; he was their special guest.

Nick saw the club was doing a thriving business. He was in Heaven. Wow! If only he could be part owner of this club, then he could make money and have all the women he wanted. So the offer was presented to Al.

"Find 50,000 dollars and you're in," Al remarked.

Well, needless to say, Nick swindled a few more people got the fifty G's and handed it to Big Al.

Within two weeks of Nick's being part owner, Al arranged for a huge bust on his strip joint and everyone landed in jail. The club was shut down for about a week then reopened with a different club name. The only difference was that Nick was no longer a part owner of a club; he was in jail doing time. Nick couldn't even make bail.

Several weeks later Al met with Susan and handed her the $50,000. She cried like a baby. "Well, Susan, this is our way of repaying you for saving our ass that afternoon in Nick's office. Quit slobbering. Go home, Kid."

Susan went home, gave her father back the money, and wondered about all the other women that Nick had swindled. She had to put Nick out of her mind.

As for Nick, he finally figured out that Al shammed him, but he wasn't going to question why. By the time he got out of jail, he was a bum. He drank and drank and drank. He knew he was worthless. So that's how Nick ended up on the streets of New York.

With his book clutched to his chest, Nick awoke from his sleep. It was early in the morning; the street was blaring with noise. He opened the book once more, just to make sure he wasn't dreaming.

"Believe"

Only you know what is best for you It's time to reach inside of you; it's time to feel your pain.

It's time to right your wrong. It's time you listen to you; Only you know what you must do. Only you know and only you can do what is right for you.

So start right now! Your road uphill will be a struggle; you will need to overcome many obstacles. You will need to go against the judgment of many people and you will need to bypass their prejudices.

You can have whatever you want if you try hard enough. Karma is your lot. It's time to right your wrong. It's time to pay your dues. Karma, Karma, Karma is for you.

Nick picked himself up, brushed himself off, and put the book into his pocket. He knew it was time for him to right his wrong. "Believe." The words in the book kept playing over and over in his mind like a broken tape. He now Believed.

Within two weeks he found a way to clean himself up. He owed hundreds of thousands of dollars, but he was determined to pay back every cent. He got himself a menial job. He made one phone call to a friend; that friend was Susan. He asked Susan if she would take him in and told her of his mission.

In spite of the past, Susan still had a soft spot for Nick and was willing to give him a second chance. Everyone deserved a chance, she thought.

Summer, Fall, Winter, Spring. Days turned into weeks and weeks turned into months. Nick in his spare time worked for the Legal Aid, helping his fellow man. This was his Karma; this was his way of righting his wrong. He knew that in time he would make good with whatever little money he had. His life was changing for the better.

Susan was at his side, taking care of all his money and making sure that the names on his list of people were paid.

She set up a non-profit organization for legal aid for the poor. While Susan gathered donations on top of donations from the rich, Nick was giving of himself in every way he could. Together they helped hundreds of people.

It was then Nick realized he must go back to the homeless. It was time that he parted with his book; it was time to pass the book on to the next person. Nick rolled his eyes up toward heaven; he had the next person in mind. Richard . . . yes.

Nick walked briskly down to the homeless compound with book in hand. He hoped he would find Richard there. Luck was on his side. Off in the distance, he could see Richard. He called out, "Hey, Richard, it's me, Nick."

Richard looked up. He was holding on to an old dirty guitar. This guitar was all that was left of Richard's past.

"Hey, where ya been, Boy. Let me look at you. Yeah." He spun Nick around. You look fine . . . got any change you could spare?"

Nick handed Richard a twenty-dollar bill.

Richard chuckled. "You must be rich, Boy."

"No, I just straightened out my life. Everything is going well now."

"How did you do that, Buddy?" Richard asked, strumming his old guitar.

"Well, I got this book from a friend, Joe. You remember him?" Nick smiled and sat down next to Richard in the gutter.

"Joe? Oh, yeah, how's he doing anyway? Book . . . what book?"

Nick handed the book "Believe" to Richard. "This book can save your life." Nick was persistent.

"Let me see." Richard felt a little tipsy as he opened the book.

"Believe"

If we Believe we will find our destiny.

Chapter 3

"Believe"

It's not too late to believe. . . . It's not to late too change your life. It's not too late to change the unthinkable. For if you believe, time will change things. . . . There is hope for the future. . . .

Believe in your heart that hope is not closing of your eyes to the difficulty of risk or failure. It is a trust that if you fail now you shall not fail forever: and if you are hurt, you shall heal. Time heals all wounds. Look at the past; know you can right your wrong.

Love yourself first and foremost. You can make things happen. You can make a difference.

It is a trust that life is good, love is powerful, and the future is full of new promises. It's time to look within. It's time to stop punishing yourself for the hurt of long ago.

It's time to let go of the bottle; it's time to live. For if you follow the spiritual steps within, your whole life *will change. Your time is running out for tomorrow may be too late.*

Whoa! Richard hung his head in shame. Nick walked off, leaving Richard time to reflect. The words he read were penetrating Richard's drunken mind. He looked up momentarily from the book "Believe;" his mind raced back in time to another place, another time. Remembering!

Richard was once a leading rock star of the nineties. Concert after concert, city after city, he was the idol of every woman both young and old. They loved his clean-cut features and deep blue eyes; his fans went crazy over his sensual movements when he sang.

Richard began drinking while on the road with his band. He had plenty of women. You might say Richard was messed up emotionally. There wasn't enough cocaine, booze or women for him in his lifetime. Until one evening when he met Candis, a beautiful natural blonde, at a typical Hollywood bash. She was sensational. He had to have her.

Candis found her way in life by taking up with men who were never emotionally there for her. She became the trophy toy: pretty, refined, always there if they wanted or needed her. Candis felt that love was the answer to all her problems.

And Richard. . . . Well, his smile was worth millions.

Women fell to their knees just to be with him. Candis was well aware of who he was and was flattered that Richard would even notice her. They talked for hours. It wasn't long before they were actively dating. Why, they were the item. *The National Inquirer* wrote stories upon stories of their love affair.

Candis felt as though she were living a fairy tale: limos, parties, drinking, meeting all the right people. Richard fell madly in love with Candis and sang to her in every audience from New York to Europe. She was flattered.

Within six month's time they moved into a luxury ten-room apartment on the exclusive side of Park Avenue. This was Richard's style. One room alone catered to his baby grand piano and its walls were filled with displays of his many awards and old guitars.

Richard and Candis spent hours together, while Richard composed hit after hit to Candis, the love of his life. They made love passionately.

Candis was different from his other ladies. She didn't drink as much as Richard did; in fact, she hardly drank at all. Days turned into months. Their love was like no other. Candis was so perfect for Richard; she was his million-dollar show piece.

Candis in her own way was working on helping Richard with his drinking problem. She knew in time he would quit. That day was near.

Richard wanted Candis to marry him; he couldn't imagine a day without her. He tapered his drinking way down, took on less gigs. He knew soon they would have their country home in Colorado . . . acres and acres of land, high up in the mountains, away from people. There would be time to reflect; time to go back to basics; time to strum on his guitar, sit back, have a couple of children, and write music again. He finally found the lady of his dreams; he found Candis.

The millennium was approaching. Richard and Candis prepared for his last concert of the year and century in the heart of New York City. Richard was looking forward to it, for after this New Year's Eve gig he'd have all the money in the world to settle down, get married, and buy his land in the mountains.

They rushed off into the limo to Times Square in New York City. Candis and Richard would announce their wedding plans to the crowd of millions who gathered for the New Year's Eve celebration and concert. This one show would be televised to millions throughout the world.

Richard made his way to center stage as the crowd came alive once more. It was electrifying. When the members of the band were introduced one by one as they appeared on stage, the crowd went wild. If you close your eyes, you can see the pandemonium that set in. Richard was used to this. There was a time he couldn't live without it. Now he could.

The number of people that gathered for this millennium celebration was beyond belief. The build-up was monumental. When Richard burst into song, there were yelling, screaming and tears.

About forty minutes into the celebration Richard asked for Candis to come join him on stage. She shyly walked out from behind the curtain. The audience cheered and screamed.

"Hold it down, Folks," Richard shouted into the mike and motioned for silence to the audience. "Hold it down. I have something to say." A hush came over the audience.

"This is Candis, Everyone. You've read about her in every newspaper. Now I want you to hear it from me. Candis will be my wife and you're all invited to the wedding. Candis, say 'hi,' Baby." Richard beamed with pride.

"Hi, Everyone," Candis said shyly and waved.

The crowd went wild once again. Richard held Candis tightly in his arms as he kissed her for the world to see. The flash bulbs from cameras burst with excitement. The fans screamed and yelled. The world was finally seeing Richard and Candis together.

Suddenly, shots rang out! Pandemonium set in. Before Richard could react, Candis fell to her knees and keeled over into Richard's arms. Candis had been shot.

"My god! Oh, my god, someone help her!" he shouted. Then he softly asked Candis, "Are you okay, Baby?"

Candis moaned. "Richard, my leg. I can't move my leg. What's happening?"

All hell broke loose by the time a medical helicopter arrived on the scene. The crowd was pushed back. This was the only way out; there was no room to drive, just wall to wall people. Richard boarded the Helicopter as it took off while several people in the audience chased the woman who fired the gun and tackled her to the ground. She turned out to be an obsessive fan madly in love with Richard.

The blare of police sirens on the ground, the whirr of helicopter rotors. The helicopter took off with Candis cradled in Richard's arms.

The medics immediately put oxygen over her mouth and tried to stop the bleeding as best as they could. One medic looked up at Richard and reassured him she was going to be all right. "She's going to live. It looks like the bullet penetrated her leg and shattered some bones, but I assure you she will pull through."

This was too much for Richard to bear. Weeks turned into months, months of major therapy. Candis slowly was able to walk with a cane; she was gaining back the use of her left leg.

Richard's drinking, however, was becoming worse. He stayed out of the public eye. Even though Candis was getting better and better every day, it seemed to him that all his dreams were crumbling. While Candis had therapy around the clock, Richard was nowhere to be found.

Within nine months he was almost forgotten. There were no concerts; he refused to work. His friends quit coming around. Richard's money was dwindling; most of it went to pay medical bills. The rest... Well, you know the rest. He drank himself sick; he drank himself into a stupor almost every night. He forgot what love was all about; the addiction of alcohol took over.

There was very little that Candis could do. She needed her therapy and several operations to get well. Until then she was helpless and dependent on him. She cried almost every night, for she wanted the love of the Richard she once knew, the sweet, loving guy she fell in love with. But he was nowhere to be found.

Richard knew he would soon lose his Park Avenue apartment. He had to break the news to Candis and it wasn't easy. One cold sober evening he spoke to her.

"Candis, I'm broke, Babe. I have about 40,000 dollars left; I want you to have it. I can't stay here anymore. You take the money for the rest of the doctor bills; this will see you through. Candis, look in my eyes. I want you to understand. You have to leave this place and so do I. You need to find a friend or someone to take care of you. I have to go."

"Richard, I love you so much. Why are you doing this to me?" she cried.

"Candis, maybe in time I will find you again, but for now I can't. I need to get away from here and you need to get away from me. I'm poison to you. Here, take the money; it's cash." Crying like a baby, he fell into Candis' lap. Always remember I love you, no matter what. Just remember I love you." Richard left the apartment.

Weeks turned into months while Richard was thrown out of every bar in New York. He ran his tab to the max. Friends didn't want anything to do with him. The next thing you know he ended up in the homeless compound . . . strumming on his old guitar. He was down to drinking old leftover bottles of wine, anything that he could find in the dumpsters of New York. He wrote songs of love and despair on discarded paper napkins, cardboard boxes, and any other material he could lay his hands on. His writing became an obsession.

Richard had been homeless for at least a year now. He found a broken mirror lying next to him on the ground; he picked up the mirror and stared long and hard into it. Then he reopened the book "Believe." A cold wind swept over the book as the pages turned.

"Believe"

As you stare at the pages in this book, look deep within your soul. Know that you're looking older, your hair looks tired and that sparkle that once shined in your eyes as a child has faded.

It's time to awaken your soul from within. Look in the mirror, my friend. That face in your mirror is changing right in front of you. Deep inside you know that this is a transition you need to face.

This is your last wake-up call. It's time to start doing the things you want to do, time to think about making changes, time to get your life in order before it's too late.

Forget your past for who you are is everything. You are the sum total of each and every thought you once had.

Change is good; life is an adventure. Look for the invisible and listen to the silences within your heart.

Your life is just starting again and by believing in change you will once again believe in yourself and everything fresh and new. All that you will be.

Richard closed the book and thought upon these words very deeply. It was as if these magical words were meant for him. He fell asleep holding the book tightly in his hands, uttering the words "believe, believe, believe. . . ."

Early the next morning he knew what he had to do . . . he found his way to Alcoholics Anonymous.

He attended meeting after meeting until he found a sponsor. Shortly thereafter, he was admitted into a center where he was in a detoxification program for several weeks.

Those were the hardest weeks of his life. There were times he didn't know if he could make it. He cried like a baby for wanting one sip of alcohol. He shook and shivered well into the night. He screamed at the top of his lungs and tried to throw things that weren't there; he slammed his head into a heavily padded wall, hoping this would put him out of his misery.

Winter turned into spring and Richard was getting better slowly. Every day and every way Richard was regaining his sanity. He rested for weeks and spent a great deal of time out on the lawn and talked with the other patients. He looked at life a little differently now. One afternoon he had a visitor for the first time in months.

Tom, one of his old band members, had read in the trades that Richard was in seclusion. For some reason, Tom knew where to find him.

"Hey, Richard. How you doing, Buddy?"

Richard gave Tom a slight smile and nodded.

"I see you're getting better. They say you can leave here within a week," Tom said.

Richard nodded again. "Yes, but I'm broke. I don't really know where to go. Can you spare a little money to help me out, Pal?" he asked.

Tom smiled. "No problem. I've been saving this check you gave me; it's still good. It's not much, but I think it will get you started. The band regrouped after you left and we're doing well again. In fact, we have a new manager and we're getting ready to cut a single. You think you might want to join up with us again, Buddy? We always have room for you."

Richard shook his head and looked it down. "No." He quickly looked up again and asked, "Tom, what happened to Candis? Have you heard anything? Is she all right?"

"Well, last I heard she moved in with a relative in some remote area. I haven't heard much, though. All I know is she was getting better and getting her life back on track," Tom replied.

"Good for her. I still love her, you know." Richard bowed his head in shame. "But I'm not good enough for her. It's better she find someone to love her like I once did." Richard lowered his head again and sobbed.

Tom was squirming; he felt helpless. He wanted to help Richard but he knew he couldn't. He handed Richard a check for $2000. He couldn't bear to see a grown man cry. "Well, Richard, I have to be going now. Keep in touch." Tom exited the grounds.

A week rolled around pretty fast and Richard felt a lot better. The evening before he left the center he opened his book "Believe" to give him courage.

"*Believe*"

Words to the wise: this road you have taken may seem uphill. Just be who you are that is wise and well.

Sharing who you are is to share yourself. Doing what you love is to do enough.

There is nothing to prove except to yourself. Never doubt who you are, for the road that you take will always be uphill.

You're never alone in your travels, for a higher power will magically appear and light your way.

Always know beyond a doubt that you are truly loved. Know this from the bottom of your heart down to your soul and your path in life will clearly be shown.

But when your path comes to an end, you will find that there is no greater joy than finding yourself again.

With this wonderful thought, Richard left the hospital and decided to take a Greyhound bus from New York to Colorado. With check in hand it was time to fulfill his dream of living in the mountains.

Several days passed. Richard had time to do a lot of thinking about his life. He knew when he got to Colorado he would find his place in the whole scheme of things.

The bus stopped abruptly in Denver. He decided to

hitch a ride higher up in the mountains to Aspen. He'd fined a place to sleep for the night, open a bank account, and settle in. And that's just what he did.

Once settled, he checked out the entertainment in the area. It seemed to be quite good.

One lazy afternoon he found himself walking along the street, gazing at the quaint stores. He came upon an old music shop and there she was, a brand new beautiful guitar. The price was well over $500, but he had to have it. He now knew how he would make a living.

Richard took the guitar to his small but quaint condo and practiced every day for hours on end. He divided his time by strumming on his guitar, composing music, and going to AA meetings to stay straight.

After several months, he felt good; he gained back a lot of his self-esteem. It was time for him to look for a job. One evening after exploring a few of the night spots, he came upon a little rustic inn with a fire place. He introduced himself to the owner of the dinner house and was well received.

The owner seemed to recognize him. "Hey, aren't you that guy from that band . . . you know, that famous person, Richard . . . what's his name?"

Richard smiled and shyly said, "Yes."

"Whatever happened to you, Boy, and what are you doing up here?"

"It's a long story. I had to take care of some things. I went into rehab and started working on my life. Well, now, here I am living my dream in Aspen."

"I can give you a gig singing here to entertain the dinner folks, but I can only give you weekends," said the owner. Then he quickly added, "But you really don't want something like this. . . . I mean, you were so famous, I'm sure you can be famous again. But I can't pay you enough money like you're used to. You know what I mean."

"Hey, Man, anything will help. I want this; this is the first time in my life I can get a fresh start. I need this real bad. I've written some songs and I just want to play my guitar. Money, I have a little. If I can get enough to pay my rent, I'll be happy," Richard said.

"Okay, Boy, I'll support you. You do get tips here; that should help you a bit. You can start this weekend for the early dinner crowd. Is 6 p.m. okay?"

"I'll be here." As Richard started to leave, he turned to the owner and smiled. "Thanks."

Back in his condo, Richard said a prayer and thanked the Lord. He was finally doing what he wanted to do: strum on his guitar, live in his head, live with his thoughts. He started a fire in the fire place; He watched the glow of the hot ambers; the fierce flames were magnificent. He sat on the floor and got comfortable, then pulled out his book.

"Believe"

Change . . . how it touches our very soul. Oh, how it can arrive at any moment in our lives, but we must not feel threatened by it or be fearful of it.

When change is upon us, we should open our eyes wider. We should extend our arms farther and embrace the world with love, for without change we would still be standing in the same spot.

Change . . . let her jolt you, push you and pull you. Let it challenge you. Know in your heart that change is what gives you the chance to be yourself. Change gives you the opportunity to make your life everything you want it to be.

Richard read these words and closed the book "Believe." He fell into a peaceful sleep.

Friday night. This would be a challenge. He had practiced several songs for the evening. He noticed his palms were sweating a little as he made his way to the dinner house with his guitar in hand.

He shook his head and said aloud, "God, give me strength to face this. Give me strength to face the booze, the crowds. Just give me strength."

Richard took his seat on a small but quaint bar stool, not quite what he was used to, but better than he had hoped for.

He picked up his guitar and started to strum a few lyrics. The audience was too busy eating and talking to notice; there was much chatter, but Richard kept plugging along.

The weeks sped by. Richard was developing a following. Word was out; they knew who he was. The crowds were getting bigger and bigger. Richard, however, just wanted to be accepted in the town; he wanted to play and be left alone. Most of the time he got his wish. He made a few friends along the way and was happier than he had been in years.

Then, one evening while strumming on his guitar, a young lady shouted out a request from the back of the room. "Hey, Richard, can you play the song 'I'm Only Happy with You'?"

"I'm sorry, Ma'am, that's from my old days. I don't play that stuff any more," he said.

"Richard, please, just for old times sake!" she shouted.

Richard glanced up from his guitar. "I told you, Lady, I don't . . . Oh, my god . . . Candis, it's you. How did you find me?"

Candis stood up from her chair in the back of the room. She grabbed her cane and walked slowly but perfectly to Richard.

Richard embraced Candis with all his heart and all his soul. "You found me, Babe. How did you find me?" he repeated.

She replied, "Merely by chance."

They both smiled. They knew their meeting wasn't by chance.

Then there was silence from the audience. Richard made sure Candis had a chair up front. He continued to play.

There was a moment when he reached into his pocket pulling up a dirty old napkin with writing on it. He held the napkin with the writing on it way up in the air and shouted, "Candis, I've been saving this song for you, My Darling."

The words he sang that night were only for her. Those words were written on his hands and knees while living in the homeless compound. He knew somewhere, someday they would meet again; and when they did, he had this very special song for her.

When his session was over, he asked Candis if she would go home with him, for they had a lot of catching up to do. Richard smiled happily when she said yes. They exited the smoky dinner house arm locked into arm together.

In his condo, he held Candis so tightly in his arms; he never wanted to let her go. They talked for hours.

He asked, "Candis, what happened to you after I left?"

"Richard, I couldn't understand why you left. I was so scared. I called my sister in upstate New York. She picked me up and I stayed with her ever since. I tried to find you, but no one knew where you were," Candis cried. "I cried every night. I wanted to be with you so badly."

Richard held her and said, "Baby, you don't have to cry any more. I'll never leave you now. How did you find me in Colorado?"

Candis wiped away her tears and explained. "Several months ago I picked up one of the trade papers. It mentioned that you were in some sort of rehab clinic in upstate New York. It also mentioned that you were going to be released soon. I figured you would come to Colorado; I knew you wanted to follow your dream. Remember? We had such dreams of this place. So I followed my hunch, knowing you could never stay away from music. And, well, here I am." She smiled.

Richard gave her a great big hug. "Thank God you remembered. To be honest with you, Candis, I wouldn't have been looking for you. I was too ashamed of myself. I didn't know how to say I was sorry. There was too much explaining to do. I just couldn't deal with it, you know."

"I understand, Richard." Candis got up and reached for her cane. "Well, I guess I better be going now."

Richard stopped her. "Going . . . where are you going? He held Candis tightly and pleaded, "Please don't leave; I need you. I promise, Babe, I won't ever let you go again. We'll work this out, I promise."

Candis said sweetly, "I'll stay. I still love you, Richard. I have but one question to ask."

"Yes?"

"How did this all come about? Why did you decide to go to rehab? How did you end up here?"

Richard smiled. "Candis, that's three questions, but who's counting. Sit down; I have something to show you."

Candis sat. Richard pulled out his book from his pocket and handed it to her.

She opened the book slowly. . . .

"*Believe*"

You are led through many lifetimes by your own spiritual guides within side of you. If you turn away from your many possible futures before you're certain you don't have anything to learn from them, then you will lose a lifetime of understanding of yourself. You always have a choice in life. There are many possible futures, so choose wisely.

"Richard, this is so beautiful," she said. "Where did you get this book 'Believe'?"

"The book was given to me by a homeless friend. It changed my life. He repeated those very words, 'It changed my life.' Richard suddenly stiffened. "I forgot something, Candis. There is only one rule in this book I didn't follow . . . I'm supposed to pass this book on. I have to go to New York; I have to give this book 'Believe' to the next person. Do you understand?"

"I guess."

"Come with me; we'll go together. Get your things. I'll make arrangements with my boss."

"Richard, I have a car you can drive to New York."

"Great, Babe, let's go."

Off they went back to the homeless camp, a trip that would take about five days. Richard wanted Candis by his side all the way.

When they arrived in New York as scheduled, Candis asked, "Richard, who are you going to give this book to?"

"Good question." Richard thought for a moment, very deeply, then snapped his fingers. "Amy, sweet Amy. There is a finer homeless lady in all of Manhattan. Come on, Candis, let's see if we can find her."

Find her they did. Amy was sitting by herself on the ground.

"Amy, it's me, Richard, and this is my lady, Candis."

Amy looked up. She was a very thin, frail young lady with blue eyes and blonde hair. She looked out of place at the homeless compound.

"Richard! I'll be, it really is you. You look good. Do you want a drink?"

"No, Amy, I don't drink anymore." He smiled at Candis.

"What happened?" Amy asked.

Richard held up the book "Believe." "It's this book. It

changed my life. You've got to read it, Darling, please. Your whole life will change."

Amy reached for the book. She opened it.

"Believe"

1. It's time to reflect upon your life.

2. Remember a time in your life when your were totally at peace with yourself. Remember how good life felt. Remember how easy your life was.

3. It's time to release the past.

4. Remember your dreams. Remember who you once were. We all have many gifts and talents bestowed upon us. It's time to reflect upon your strengths, not your weaknesses All you have to do is believe in yourself, and I promise your whole life will change.

Let Go

You cannot erase the past; so let go. You must learn from your mistakes. You cannot stop time or even stand still in this world. Flow with the wind.

Let the shadows of the past be gone. Let love in. It's time to make your move. It's time to face the future of life. For new doors are waiting to be opened. Come out and play, take a chance, for a new future is awaiting you.

Amy closed the book with tears in her eyes. She looked up at Richard and asked "Can I keep this book for a while?"

Richard smiled and held on to Candis' hand. "Yes, Amy, keep reading, for your whole life is about to change." Richard walked away slowly with Candis so as not to disturb Amy as she continued to read on.

"Believe"

Life is a gift Dreams are made in Heaven

Chapter 4

"Believe"

Amy sat in a crouched position, tightly clutching her new book "Believe" to her chest. She reflected on the words that were written and she thought briefly how good Richard looked.

She wondered how a book could change your life. She had heard about Joe. Was it really possible for a book to change your thinking? She felt as though there was a message in what she had read. Just to feel the words once more, Amy opened the book again.

"Believe"

It's never too late to change. At anytime you can decide to change the road you're on. You are the captain of your ship. You are the only one who really knows what you want from life.

You're the one who knows which road to take. Many roads are filled with pitfalls; we call these roads of knowledge, roads of understanding, roads of destiny.

For if we never experience a pitfall we would never learn life's greatest challenges and gifts.

You are the only one who can fulfill your dreams and receive the happiness that comes from reaching your greatest heights.

Just like a pianist in the beginning, learning the scale on the piano is so hard to memorize but as time goes by the pianist plays wonderful, beautiful music.

Life can be that hard and that easy. Don't expect others to be responsible for your happiness. It's time to take control of your destiny. For life is one great journey into the unknown.

Well, that did it. Amy read words that were written for her. She knew this book was special. She knew this book could help her change her life.

How could a random book know that she once played the piano? She shook her head in disbelief, She remembered how happy she once was when playing the piano. "I don't get it, but maybe it's time for me just to believe."

Amy thought back to when she was eight years old and living in upstate New York with her middle-class parents. One bright morning a piano was delivered to her house. Her mother wanted Amy to learn how to play the piano;

she felt that every child should learn a musical instrument. Amy couldn't believe her eyes.

"Is that for me, Mom?" she asked with excitement.

"Yes, Baby. I was taught the piano when I was your age. I thought you would like to learn how to play."

"Oh, Mom, can I try? Please teach me! I want to learn." Amy could barely contain her excitement.

Her mom sat down on the piano stool and motioned for Amy to sit next to her while she played a romantic classical piece.

Amy was mesmerized. She turned to her mother and said, "Mom, that was beautiful."

As the weeks went by, Amy lived to play the piano. Each day after school she couldn't wait to race home to practice on the piano.

Her mother noticed that Amy was catching on extremely fast for a normal child of 8 years old. She decided to hire a professional piano teacher. As the weeks turned into months, Amy's obsession over the piano was becoming evident. Her teacher threw increasingly difficult pieces at her, yet nothing seemed that hard or that difficult for Amy to learn.

One Christmas Eve Amy gazed out of her living room window at the drifting silent snow as she played the piano in a trance-like state.

Her mother, busy in another room, suddenly and most

unexpectedly heard the most astounding piece of music. She thought for a moment that it was a Rachmaninoff piece. No, that couldn't be. The music grew louder and louder as her mother made her way into the living room. She couldn't believe what she was hearing. Amy was playing classical music on her own. Her mother waited patiently till Amy was through.

Amy gazed over at her mother and smiled. "Did you like it, Mom?"

"How . . . Where did you learn that?" her mother asked.

"My teacher was practicing this piece. I thought it was beautiful, so every day I practiced a little till finally I was playing it on my own." Amy threw her hands up in the air as if it were a fact.

It was then Amy's mother knew she was special. Within weeks her mother and father got the best of everything for this child. They hired all the right people, who tested Amy in every conceivable manner. They concluded that Amy was more than gifted; she was a child protege.

Was this a past life energy or was it genetic? The mother was very good at the piano but nothing upon nothing compared to Amy's gift.

As years went by, Amy was asked to appear on a nationally televised concert in New York and was also asked to cut her first CD for a national record company. Amy was offered scholarship after scholarship and was accepted into The Julliard School of music. Her family was amazed by all this notoriety; they knew she was gifted, but this was a bit much.

Amy, in concert, wore a black velvet dress, her long blonde hair tied back into a bun to highlight her lovely white porcelain face.

She sat at her piano and in the background an orchestra of violins played. Amy chose a beautiful concerto by Rachmaninoff. The audience was astounded. The applause was overwhelming. This particular concert was being televised all over the United States. When the concert was over the applause was monumental.

Flowers were thrown on the stage as she bowed so graciously. Her dressing room was filled with the aroma of roses.

A young man approached Amy and introduced himself. He was tall, nicely built with brown wavy hair and piercing green eyes. He had a smile that could launch ships. Charisma to the max.

"Hi, my name is Eric Petersen, Amy, you were wonderful and so very talented. I represent a company in New York, Petersen and Petersen. We're a noted talent agency and, Darling, I want to represent you and take you to the top." He smiled.

Amy couldn't take her eyes off this fast-talking young man. He was so handsome. "I would love to," she said, "but my parents handle my career. I think you will have to talk to them." She smiled shyly.

"No problem, Young Lady. I have a contract here in my hands. All you have to do is sign on the dotted line and your fame begins." He smiled again.

Amy introduced Eric to her parents and told them the news. They set up a meeting with him for Monday in his office. Meanwhile, they would have their family attorney go over the contract.

Eric was so suave, maybe a little too suave. He seemed to mesmerize Amy with his voice. Amy couldn't take her eyes off him. He bowed and kissed her hand.

"I hope I see more of you, Darling," he said.

"Thank you. I'm sure you will." She smiled.

Monday morning rolled around and all met in the office of Petersen and Petersen. The facts were laid out for the family on how they would handle Amy's career. Her family was very cautious; they wanted to think about it for a while and they would get back to Eric.

Eric boldly asked if he could take Amy out to dinner that evening. The parents felt it was okay for now. Amy was in heaven. This would be her first date in nineteen years.

She was like a child at home trying to get ready and look proper at the same time. Her parents were a little worried. Eric was about five years older; he knew the ropes. Amy was young, fresh and new. They didn't want anything or anyone to spoil her success. They knew what love could do to this child; but she was older now and could make her own decisions in life. They gave her their blessing for the evening.

Amy was dressed beautifully in a pale pink dress, a black lace choker and black heels. Her blonde hair flowed to her shoulders as she walked. Eric picked her up in his Jaguar. They were ready to head off to an elegant night on the town.

When they reached the restaurant, they were greeted by the maitre'd. "Well, hello, Mr. Petersen. We have your usual private booth waiting. My, you are coming up in the world. The lady is lovely. Why don't you both follow me."

And they did. The waiter handed a menu to Amy as well as to Eric. Amy put her menu down, stared into Eric's eyes and said, "Eric, you order for me, please."

Eric was impressed. Amy was so beautiful he couldn't take his eyes off her. The dinner was more than a success. When Eric dropped Amy at home he kissed her very gently on the cheek and told her he would call her soon.

Now, mind you, Eric was not one to fall in love with. He had many women. One woman was never enough for him. Eric was a typical playboy, a womanizer. He worked for his father to support his habit of fast cars and fast money. He worked to play. Amy was just another account to him.

Yet there was something special about her. She was young, beautiful, and very naive. That was refreshing. Most of the other ladies he dated were sexual. It was a two-way street; he wanted sex, they wanted his power. Amy was different.

Eric called Amy for several dates. They went out on a semi-regular basis, though not exclusively in his eyes. Eric wasn't about to be tied down by one woman, at least not yet.

Amy practiced her piano playing and her concertos. This was her life; Eric came second. She wasn't in love with him yet.

Her family decided they wanted an older and more respectable talent company to handle Amy, so they passed on Petersen and Petersen.

That didn't stop Eric from seeing Amy. He knew she was talented and he wanted her as a client. In fact, his father was on his case to get her signed at all costs. Eric's father didn't want her as a daughter-in-law; he wanted her as a client, and he made that very clear to Eric. There would be a hefty bonus if he signed her. Eric kept plugging along. He used all of his charisma.

Flowers, candy, music and sweet talk, Amy was beginning to fall in love with this young man. The only problem was Eric was never in love with Amy. Whenever he dropped her off at home, he opened his black book and called the next girl who was on his list. It was doubtful if Eric could ever fall in love with anyone, for money was his god.

Amy played in concert after concert. She was absolutely brilliant. Eric was always by her side. He knew one way or other he would land this account, even if he had to marry her. Amy was the biggest challenge of his life.

Amy's parents were oblivious to all this. They were concerned with her career. They liked Eric and thought he was good for her, but they never expected them to marry.

It was a hot summer day in June. Eric and Amy decided to go on a picnic by a lake in upstate New York. The sun was shining so brightly. Eric spread out the picnic blanket, opened the picnic basket, and handed Amy a crystal wine glass. He poured the wine carefully, for they were toasting their first anniversary of dating. Eric reached over to Amy and kissed her. He had his speech prepared for months.

Eric gently reached for Amy's hand and said, "Amy, I love you so much, I can't imagine my life without you. We are so perfect for each other. Will you marry me?"

Amy smiled so shyly. "Eric, I love you, too. I love you so much, but I've been holding back. I thought you really didn't love me," she said.

"Amy, I don't want to go through my life without you. You give me a reason to live. Just say you will be my wife."

"Yes, Eric, I will marry you."

"Great! Let's plan the wedding, then we can tell our folks."

Eric and Amy sat on their blanket in the park planning their wedding. Eric wanted everything to be so elaborate. He wanted to invite all of New York society. And Amy just went along for the ride.

Eric decided he would taper down on his women; he didn't want any mistakes. He didn't want to lose Amy now, not after all the hard work that he had put forth. He decided he would give it a go. He would be a good husband.

Amy worked so hard that she never knew Eric really was the playboy that she heard about. She figured when he met her, that would all be behind him. She never gave a thought to all the rumors that she heard. Besides, in her own way, her love for Eric was second to the love she had for the music she created for the world.

They couldn't wait to reach her parents' home. Amy told her mother and father. They were pleased. They wanted Amy to have a complete life and they knew that Eric would never stop her from playing the piano.

Wedding plans were in the making. They decided to have a wedding in September. There wasn't much time now. Invitations were sent out, all the arrangements were being made, and everyone who was anyone would attend this gala wedding. The church picked was on Fifth Avenue. The wedding reception would be at the Plaza Hotel.

Between the two families there must have been five hundred people invited. But everything was on schedule. Eric and Amy seemed happy.

Amy was getting fitted for her wedding dress while Eric was attending every bachelor party that was thrown for him. Why, it took one whole day for Eric to call every lady who was in his big black book to let her know he would be out of circulation for a while.

The wedding day would soon be here; the hustle and bustle would soon be over. Eric decided he had to play this straight and give marriage a chance. He needed to do this for himself.

The wedding day was finally here. Press releases were all sent out and camera crews were ready to roll.

Amy walked down the aisle in her beautiful white lace dress flowing to the ground, for all the world to see. Eric was handsomely dressed in a black tuxedo.

The priest stood in white at the podium. As he closed the Bible, he spoke those famous words: "I now pronounce you man and wife. You may kiss the bride." He smiled.

Eric kissed the bride and the music began. They danced the first dance with each other. The night was endless; it was a fairy tale.

Amy's father asked Eric to follow him into a private room.

"Have a seat, My Son. I want to congratulate you. Here, have a cigar," he requested.

Eric reached for the cigar and lit it, puffing on his cigar in a very proud fashion.

"Eric, I have a special gift for you. I know you will take care of my daughter." He spoke sternly. "Well, Son, I also know how badly you wanted to manage her career. When I first met you, I was skeptical of you, but after getting to know you I feel confident now that you will take real good care of my Amy. My gift to you, Son, is Amy."

Eric looked puzzled. "But, Sir, I married Amy. I don't get it. I already have her."

"Eric, here's a contract signed, sealed, and delivered. You now have full control of Amy's career." He smiled.

Eric was not expecting this so soon. He had known Amy's father would come around eventually but this was the icing on the cake. He now had it all. He could do whatever he wanted with Amy and her career. He had full control.

"Thank you, Sir. This was totally unexpected. You know I will value this and guide her all the way to the top. You will be proud of me. You wait and see. I will be very good to her." Eric shook hands with Amy's father.

"Well, I guess we'd better be getting back to your wedding. Shall we?"

Eric made his way back to the wedding reception. He

danced every dance with Amy till the wedding party dissipated. He told Amy the news. She was so happy that her husband would be handling her. Now she knew this marriage was forever.

They took a short honeymoon in Las Vegas. While there Eric checked out all the places that Amy would perform. Hotel after hotel . . . why, it was endless. Eric struck a few deals.

Amy was excited. She knew Eric loved her and was doing this for her. At least, that's what she told herself.

When they got home Eric mentioned to Amy that it would be wonderful if they moved to Las Vegas. This could be their big break.

Amy agreed. She said to Eric, "I'll do whatever it takes to make you happy."

"Then pack your bags, Babe. We're moving to Las Vegas." Eric was happy.

They moved to Vegas and rented a beautiful home for $3000 per month. Eric made sure Amy had a big white baby grand piano. They had all the flash and glitter that Amy's money could buy. Eric felt this was necessary to attract all the right people. They had a different party every night while Amy performed for all the bigwigs. Eric threw the parties gallantly, while Amy played the piano night after night.

Each night was a gala event. The champagne would

flow; Amy would perform; Eric would mingle. Eric landed job after job for Amy. Their bank account was growing by leaps and bounds. Amy worked to the point of sheer exhaustion. When Eric noticed that Amy was tired, he would make a point of pampering her, spending time with her just so she would perform for him even more.

One morning while they were lying in bed, Amy turned to Eric and said, "Eric, I want to spend more time with you. I want to have a baby."

"Amy, what do you mean? We're together all the time. A baby? Not now. We don't have time for a baby; you have a career to maintain," he said.

"Well, when can we have a baby? I want a real life. I want to spend time with you alone, not with all those people around us, Eric. We have plenty of money," she said.

"Amy, we'll have a child in a few years. Now is the time we make our mark, Young Lady. You're not getting any younger. We have to strike while you're fresh and hot. Right now we have all the entertainment directors eating out of our hands. Don't you see, Babe, this is it. We're headed for the big time. Just a year or so and, Babe, we'll have it all." Eric was cocky.

"You promise . . . one year?" she asked.

"Yes," he said.

Amy decided to do everything that Eric wanted. She

worked so hard in that year that her health began to fail. Eric saw that she was getting run down, so he whisked her off on a nice vacation. They stayed in Florida for a week while she regained her strength.

They spent a lot of time in bed. This felt like a real vacation for the first time since they were married. Amy played at the beach; Eric wined her and dined her. Amy looked great then. Eric decided it was time to head back to Vegas.

Amy went back to playing the piano and performing. One evening she felt dizzy. She passed out and was rushed to the hospital. After a complete examination, she found out she was pregnant.

Eric sat with her in the hospital.

"Eric, I'm pregnant," Amy said.

"I know."

"Eric, I want this baby," she said.

"Let's talk when we get home, okay?" he said.

Talk they did. Eric convinced Amy to have an abortion. He told her there would be plenty of time to have a baby, that the timing now wasn't right. He promised her that if she gave up this child and aborted the fetus, within two years they would have several children.

Amy didn't want to lose Eric, so she did as he asked. It was a tough time for Amy. She was so naive she had never known another man but him. Amy was scared. She was an abused wife. Eric controlled every situation and made all the decisions for her.

Well over a year went by. The only time Amy had to herself was when she took long walks in the park. She loved nature; she loved beauty. She would spend time reading a book. This was a peaceful time for her; she had time for herself.

Amy was growing restless with her life with Eric, but she loved to play the piano. She was growing tired of Eric. She watched the relationships of some of her friends and knew her own relationship with Eric was not healthy. She felt as though Eric never loved her. They had a business relationship and Eric controlled all the money.

Whenever Eric felt he was losing Amy, he made sure he paid just enough attention to her. This time, not even the little attention he paid to her was working. She was growing more and more restless. Eric noticed that she started to cancel more and more of her piano engagements due to illness. There was arguing in the house such as there never had been before.

Amy sank deeper and deeper into her own little world, one of lack of self esteem and self-worth.

Eric would rant and rave, yell and scream, and order Amy back to work. He called her a worthless bitch. He told her that her fans were waiting . . . how could she do this to them.

This time none of Eric's ploys worked. Amy stood up for her rights. Amy stared at Eric very intensely and firmly after a huge argument. Amy had enough; her belly was full.

"Eric, it's just not working out!" she shouted. "I want out of this relationship." She ran to her room to pack her bags.

Eric followed her. "What do you mean you want out? Look at everything I've done for you, you ungrateful bitch. I don't want to hear it. You can't walk out on me." Eric reached for Amy and shook her.

That was the last straw. Amy couldn't take it any more. She broke loose from Eric.

"Eric, I've had it with you! I never want to see you again!" she screamed.

Off she ran as fast as she could with her purse in hand. She hailed a cab and somehow made it to the Las Vegas airport.

Amy realized Eric had enabled her for so many years she didn't even know how to write a check He did everything for her. She was sad and pathetic. She managed to find a credit card in her purse and charged a ticket to New York. She was headed toward home. She had to tell her mother and father. It wouldn't be easy. She felt like a begging dog making its way home after starving for a week.

It was late in the evening when she made it back to New York and rang the doorbell of her parents' home.

Somewhat surprised, her mom and dad answered. "Amy, what are you doing here?" they asked.

Amy burst into tears. "Mom, I hate him, I hate him!" she screamed.

Her mother reached for her and comforted her.

"I never want to see Eric again. All he cares about is my career. Mom, I swear I'll never play another note on the piano; I hate the piano; I hate what Eric did to me." She cried like a baby in her mother's lap.

Her mother stroked Amy's hair. "You don't have to go back to him. It's okay. Why don't you go upstairs and take a nice hot bath," she said.

In the weeks to come Eric sent flowers; he called the house nonstop. He had to have Amy back. But she wasn't having any of that. Her parents kept insisting that she should try one more time with Eric . . . to seek counseling. Maybe things would get better; they would work out.

Amy was strong in her beliefs. "No, I hate him. All he wants me to do is play the piano so he can collect my paycheck. You just don't get it, Mom. I loved the piano with all my heart and soul. Eric made me hate what I loved so much. I will never ever play the piano again as long as Eric's around. When I'm old and gray, I'll play; but I'll play for me, not for him. I think I've overstayed my welcome here. I have to grow up sometime. Now's a good time. I've got to get away from everyone. Sorry, I'll keep in touch." She ran out the door. Amy ran so fast and never looked back, for she knew her parents would bring Eric back into her life. So she kept on running.

Weeks turned into months. Amy ran out of money. She started to live her life in all the old piano bars. She played for small fees just so she could have a drink and forget her troubles. She dropped off the planet.

Before too long she was confused, tired and hungry. She tried the Salvation Army for a while, and before long she found comfort in the homeless compound.

She was so young. She had the whole world at her feet but in her mind she would rather eat dog food before she would go back home to Eric. She felt safe in the homeless compound, for it was the one place that no one would ever think to find her.

Eric searched and searched for Amy. He hired a private detective, along with her family, but they came up empty. He was on the verge of giving up. Eric sought help; he went to a shrink. He did everything, but he knew that Amy was lost forever.

So that's how Amy ended up in the homeless compound. She wanted to change her life; she wanted to find love and move on. In the compound she made many good friends but all along she was trying to make a decision. So she picked up her book "Believe" one more time. In her heart she turned to a page and this is what it said.

"Believe"

If you're struggling to make a decision in life, give it the "old-rocking-chair" test. Close your eyes and imagine that you're ninety years old, sitting at home in your favorite rocking chair, rocking away.

As you think back upon your life, will you regret doing this? Or not regret doing this?

Pick the decision you can live with and have no regrets. Believe in your choices, then act upon them. . . .

It's time to face the world. . . . It's time to go back over your life and decide what you will do. All you have to do is Believe . . . and all things are possible.

Amy thought deeply upon the words she read. She closed the book "Believe." Her decision was made. "It's time I grow up. It's time I face the world. It seems like I have to start cleaning up my life and taking control."

Amy dusted herself off. She decided she was going to pay her mother and father a visit for she had a lot to say. It was late evening when she reached their home. Amy rang the doorbell. Her mother answered the door.

"Amy, my god, it's you! Oh, my god, I can't believe it's really you. We thought you were dead. Come in, Baby. Where have you been these last few months?" she asked.

"Mom, Dad, I came here to talk to you." Her parents were all ears. "I was living by myself. I ended up with hardly any food. I stayed with the homeless and learned a good lesson. I learned how to take care of me. It took months of thinking and growing, until a friend passed this book to me. This book changed my life. The book is called 'Believe.'" Amy paused.

Her mother and father were cautious. They didn't know if she was mentally ill or just plain crazy, so they sat and listened to her story.

"Mom, I want my life back," she cried. "I am very talented and I have so much to give. I want to help the poor. I want to play the piano for the under- privileged. What I learned most in life is not about making money. It's about feeling good inside. Feeling good about yourself. Mom, let me read to you and Dad what's in this book. This book is so wonderful," she said.

They listened.

"Mom, here, take this book. Open up to a page, any page."

Her mother humored her and opened up the book "Believe."

"Believe"

Destiny. There comes a time in your life that if you stand still, you will remain at that point forever. You realize if you fall and stay down life will pass you by.

The road to life is not always what you might want or wish for. There are times you might be led in different directions.

It's time you put effort into choosing your path; it's time you carry out your dreams.

Know in your life there is a path before you now. Rid yourself of your confusion. The past is yesterday. The future is now. Take one step at a time.

Gain your self-esteem back. Take one day one step at a time and soon you will see your future unfold right before your very eyes, and all it took was for you to Believe. . . .

Her mother couldn't believe what Amy had read. The words were so beautiful. She looked at her father and they both agreed they would support Amy in every way they could. "Amy, why don't you go upstairs and take a hot shower. We will help you."

While Amy was taking a shower, the doorbell rang. It was Eric. The family filled him in on what was happening. Eric couldn't believe what he heard.

When Amy came down from her shower she was faced with Eric to deal with. One thing Amy learned in the homeless compound: when you clean up your mess, clean it all up.

"Eric, what are you doing here?"

"I came over to talk to you. Your father called me."

Amy stared intensely at her father to make a point. "Why?"

Eric said, "Amy, you drove us nuts. We all love you so much. I am so glad you're back. Look, Amy, I want you back. I've changed. You can do whatever you want now. I promise I will support you. Come here, Baby." He opened his arms to her.

Amy stayed strong. "Eric, I don't want you back. You are a self-centered egomaniac. You have no feelings for anyone but yourself. When you shook me that was the last straw. I'd rather live out of a garbage can than live with you. And that's what I did. I want you out of my home and I want a divorce. Just get out of my sight!" she screamed.

"I wasted enough energy on you and you're not even worth it." This took a lot for a once shy Amy to say.

Amy's mom didn't say a word. She didn't want to lose Amy again. She asked Eric to leave. He got up in a huff and slammed the door.

"Thank you, Mom."

"Amy, what are you going to do?"

Mom, I want to play the piano again. I will set up a foundation to help the homeless. I will play everywhere and anywhere I can. Whatever it takes I will do it. I will donate to the homeless, feed them, help them. That's what I want to do. That's what I'm going to do. Just keep Eric away from me and I will stay here and be happy." Amy sat down, relieved.

Her mom and dad didn't quite understand, but they held their child and all had a good cry.

"I'll start tomorrow. I have so much to do now," Amy said. "Mom, I just remembered I have to go back to the homeless compound. I have to pass this book on."

"Amy, can't you do this tomorrow?"

"No, Mom. I'll be back in a few hours. Let me borrow your car."

Amy bolted out the front door with book in hand, She drove for two hours until she reached the homeless compound.

She thought out loud, "I have to give this book to someone. I know . . . I'll give the book to Jamie; she really needs the help." With book in hand she got out of the car, and there was Jamie.

"Hey, Jamie, how are you doing?"

Jamie looked up. "Hey, Amy, I thought you left here. Are you back here to stay?"

"No, Jamie. I came here to give you a book."

"A book?"

"Yes, here. The book is called 'Believe.' This book will change your life."

"Let me see." Jamie opened the book slowly and she read the words in "Believe."

"*Believe*"

Whatever you do or dream you can live it. Just Believe and the power and magic will appear.

Nothing can bring you peace but you. Life is an adventure. It's time you stop feeling sorry for yourself. It's time to Believe.

"Amy, these words are beautiful. I understand. I think I need to read more," she said.

"Jamie, follow the path and remember all you have to do is Believe." Amy walked to her car while Jamie read on.

"Believe"

Don't be frightened of change, for at the end that is all
we know.

Chapter 5

"Believe"

Never let go of your dreams. There are times when it seems our dreams are crumbling in our hands; we think that we have failed in life, that what we once tried so hard to obtain is now out of our reach and out of our dreams.

Just because we failed, this won't destroy our dreams. It's time to keep trying, no matter what.

Ignore those who try to discourage you. Keep trying, no matter what it takes.

Hold on to your dreams. Believe in yourself, for you hold the power to make things happen. As long as you keep on believing and acting upon your dreams, they will come true.

These words were so powerful to Jamie. She was only thirty years old, but there was a time Jamie had the world at her feet. She was once a high powered secretary for a computer company in the Silicon Valley.

Jamie was on her way up in life. Her company allowed her to take computer courses; she was advancing right and left. An average day would be for her to come into the office and work from 6 a.m. till 5 p.m. She also learned how to invest in the stock market, required learning for her job.

After work she would meet some of the other girls in the company at a local coffee house for drinks and appetizers. There were many computer nerds there, each brilliant in his or her own right and extremely special.

This generation of kids was different; they were the offspring of the children of the sixties. The sixties was a rough era . . . wars, crimes, riots, drugs, gas shortages, etc. It was not a peaceful era. The baby boomers were not concerned with money. They were concerned with living life and the quality of life. Pollution was a major concern and health and longevity were a quest. These priorities were passed on to their children.

But children of the sixties generation were lost. There were no more wars to fight; peace and freedom prevailed.

This new generation was extremely money oriented. When the stock market went crazy, these kids had it made. Take a few computer courses, move to the valley, and get a job working with computers, watch the stock market, invest . . . sky's the limit.

In the late eighties most of these kids had more money

than they knew what to do with. This generation created more millionaires in their twenties and thirties than one could ever imagine in this lifetime. The younger generation was putting the older generation back in the work force. Many middle-aged men and women were coming out of retirement and going back to work for the money was flowing like wine.

The boom happened all over the country The young ones bought houses and cars with cash. Cash was the name of the game. They felt safe. Jamie was part of this group. There wasn't anything these kids couldn't have or afford.

Money and the stock market dominated the conversations. A typical conversation went like this:

"Did anyone buy AOL today? What's it doing? What about Microsoft? Is it up or down? Anyone for a mocha? When's our next trip to Tahoe? I heard the skiing is great. Let's plan our next vacation somewhere exotic."

These kids never knew poverty. Talking about the homeless just wasn't allowed. Jamie and her friends never thought they could end up in a homeless camp. Why, that was only for crazy people, not for people like Jamie and her friends.

What they didn't understand was that each and every one of us, at any given time, could end up homeless. One earthquake, fire, national disaster could send us all for a loop.

Jamie and her friends refused to believe in anything but the stock market. It was the endless pit of wealth for America. Invest, invest, put all your money in the market, buy, sell, exchange, day-trade. So you lose a few, you gain a few; learn the game and soon you will be a millionaire.

This was the philosophy of this 1999-2000 generation. Jamie was learning the market by leaps and bounds. She was quite good at it. She started with $1000 and parlayed it into $5000 before long. The main theme of the day was "Well, how much money did you make today?" Jamie's friend, Matt, would ask that question on a regular basis.

Jamie felt inferior to some of her friends who had millions and still worked for the company in Silicon Valley merely out of sheer boredom. They stayed on just to monitor their stocks in the company.

Although Jamie was attractive . . . red hair, green eyes, slender figure . . . she didn't have much of a social life; in fact, hardly any at all for she was way too busy. She didn't have time to socialize with men; instead, she buried her head in books, learning the market and studying computer technology.

Her main goal in life was to be a millionaire by age 32 and she was on her way. She studied the market like no other, watching the trends, listening to the analysts and watching for the dips in the market. Buying, selling, trading. . . .

She didn't have patience for trading long and waiting like other people. She preferred day trading, the quick fix. By summer's end, she had well over $20,000, saved. Jamie was so pleased.

She moved out of her parent's home and found herself a nice apartment in the Silicon Valley, pricey but nice. The rent was $1500 per month for a small one-bedroom.

Jamie was part of the groupies; she was accepted. This group of nerds was fascinating. There was James, a high powered computer nerd. Brandon, who dealt with the stock market exclusively; and Katie, who researched the market for the group. These were Jamie's new best friends. They ate together, partied together, and played together.

Investing was their game. They hardly had time to date. The best that could be expected was dinner and a movie. They had a common goal: money and lots of it. They all wanted to work hard at achieving goals and they devoted many hours to researching the market. In time they knew they would all be quite wealthy. Their fun times would be searching for new homes or buildable lots in the area; much of the land to be found was on slopes overlooking the ocean.

Jamie had but one parent, her father. Her mother died of cancer, and her father never married again. Most of the time he lived alone in his small studio apartment. It was only on rare occasions that he had time for Jamie, his only child. They really had very little in common.

Most of her years were spent being shuffled around to and from distant relatives. She remembered a time in her life when she and her dad were so poor they once had to live at the Salvation Army's shelter.

That was behind her now. She often repeated a line by Scarlet O'Hara from the movie "Gone With The Wind:" "As God is my witness I will beg, steal and borrow, but, I shall never go hungry again." Jamie never ever wanted to be poor. She was going to make something of herself, and she did.

She was very proud of herself. She felt she was more than making it. A typical day for Jamie was waking up at 4 a.m. and going to the 24-hour gym to work out before making her way down the street to her office. There would be notes from her boss telling her what to do, which she followed to a tee.

She always turned on the stock market to monitor her stocks as well as her boss's. Her other computer allowed her to day trade on a moment's notice.

One particular day her stocks were rallying straight up. She was buying and selling at a feverish pace. Within 15 minutes she had made $20,000. Whoa! this was unheard of. She put out an office memo to Brandon and Katie, her office buddies, and faxed them the great results of her stock picks for the day. She hoped they would all jump on board. And they did. By day's end they were all $20,000 richer.

By the end of the day they had decided to go to San Francisco for a shopping spree. It was quitting time, but they still had time to hit all the great stores: electronics, digital cameras, video digital cameras, dvd's and home entertainment stores. They shopped till they dropped. And they topped it off with a glass of Merlot at a local after-hours hangout.

Next on their grand list of things to do was a trip to Maui with Martin Luther King's birthday coming up. They bought first class tickets to the islands. Maui was only five hours away from San Francisco. Once on board, they had a ball.

When they landed in Honolulu, they took a quick twenty-minute flight on Aloha Airlines to Maui. They rented a convertible and sang all the way into Lahaina. First class was the name of the game.

Maui was beautiful. They took surfing lessons; one went para sailing, while the others went wave riding. They danced till the wee hours of the morning and sun bathed all day. They did know how to live. They lived for today, never caring about tomorrow. The money pit was endless, so they thought. By Sunday evening they really, needed a vacation.

It was time to head back to the Bay Area. Tuesday they would have to face the real world once again. Besides, it was important to get up early and watch the markets open. And that they did. Within a six-month period of time this lucky-streak seemed to be never ending. Jamie now had well over $150,000. Not bad for a small buy in. Life was good.

It was October when her luck started to change. The market turned. There was much talk of Alan Greenspan's raising the interest rates. The market was like a roller-coaster. Up 200 points in one day, down 500 points the next.

This wouldn't have been bad for a person who was trading for the long term. If you trade for the long term or retirement, you leave your money in, no matter what, for the market will eventually go back up.

When you're a day-trader, you trade every day. Some take all their money out by day's end. Others play. That's exactly what Jamie did. She played.

Brandon and Katie were smarter. By day's end they pulled their money to cut their losses, if there were any. They warned Jamie on many occasions. But Jamie thought she knew it all; she couldn't lose.

That October the stock market went crazy; pandemonium set in. Jamie tried like hell to pull her money out, but her stocks were in a nose dive. With day-trading, if everyone is selling at a fast pace, there are times your sell orders can stack up, waiting for 15 minutes or more to sell. Now, in this day and age, fifteen minutes in the market could be a lifetime . . . good, bad or indifferent. By the time Jamie pulled her money out, she had a mere $2000 left.

Jamie was devastated. She ran to the ladies's room and started heaving. She was an emotional wreck. Then in walked Katie.

"Jamie, what's wrong? Do you have the flu or something?" she asked.

Jamie glanced up blankly. "I lost all my money, Katie. I only have 2000 dollars left. I lost it all," Jamie cried.

Katie needed to find out exactly what Jamie did wrong. "Girl, what's the matter with you! Brandon and I watched the market; we pulled our money out. Chalk it up to a bad day; there's always tomorrow. Why are you sweating it, Girl?"

"You don't understand. I lost everything. I mean I only have 2000 dollars left and that's not enough to play with," she said.

Katie shook her head with disgust. She couldn't believe what she was hearing. "You mean, you lost over 148,000 dollars?"

"Yes!" she cried.

"Oh, my god, why didn't you stop?" Katie asked.

"I tried, but the market was going crazy." Jamie cried, shaking her head in shame.

Katie felt a little bit of sympathy for Jamie and Put her

head on her shoulder. "Why don't you go home early and relax. Get a grip, Girl. Think it through."

Jamie did just that. She went home, took a nice hot bath and thought it through. She spoke out loud to herself. "I'm not going to give up this easily. I'll make some money in the morning." She drank a glass of Merlot and fell fast asleep in the bathtub.

The next day the market was a little bit kinder. She invested her $2000 and made $4000. She was on a roll again. Jamie was determined to get her money back. By week's end she had $10,000 dollars in her account. "I guess I worried for nothing. The market is recovering." Jamie ate, drank and slept for the love of the market. There was never enough money in the market for her to gain. She was flying high once more.

Jamie felt $10,000 dollars wasn't enough to play the market. She was now investing in the bigger stocks such as AOL and IBM, whose stocks start trading for at least $90 per share on up. These stocks were considered safe. She needed more money. She thought out loud, "Where can I get money from fast? I know!" She pulled out her credit cards and stared at them. "I know I shouldn't be doing this, but I have a feeling the market's going to take off. I need lots of money to buy in."

So Jamie broke the cardinal rule: Don't use your credit cards for stock purchase. Well, she did. She borrowed the max on each card, which came to a total of $20,000. All that she had left in this world.

Of course she thought she would just borrow the money for six months at a low interest rate. Jamie believed with all her heart and soul she would gain back the money and pay off the credit cards in full way before her six months deadline.

The next morning bright and early Jamie bought into the market for $20,000. Early in the morning things looked great; the market was in an uphill trend. But all did not go as planned. Later in the day the market turned. Her stocks were nose-diving once again. Alan Greenspan had just made his predictions for the coming month: slight inflation, a rate hike of 1/2 percent. That's when the market went crazy "My god, I've got to get out of this," she said. She tried as hard as she could to sell her stocks. But all was lost, every single dime that Jamie had invested.

That was it; she was tapped out. She went home that evening and cried like a baby. She had only two thousand dollars left, just enough to pay her last month's rent and catch up. She would have to vacate her apartment. As for work, she had to get out of there. She couldn't face Brandon and Katie. Her job revolved around the stock market. She felt she didn't have a choice. She had nowhere to go. To make a long story short, that's how Jamie ended up in the homeless camp.

Jamie was mentally ill at this point; she babbled a lot. She held the book "Believe" tightly in her hands as she read a page out loud.

"Believe"

Keep looking for the peace in life that you are searching for. Keep believing that life holds new promise for you. Keep trying to be all that you can be. Don't give up; don't give in. For in your heart you know you can be the winner deep inside of you.

Remember the magic in life when you feel you have reached the end of your rope. Let whatever mistakes you have made remain in your past as shadows of days gone by. It's time to pick yourself up off the ground and brush yourself off, for tomorrow is a bright new day.

The words she read were heart throbbing. They touched the very core of her soul.

Jamie knew what she must do now. She had spent only a few weeks in the homeless camp. But that was more than enough time for her to come to a realization.

So she picked herself up from the gutter and brushed herself off. She held her head high as she walked out of the homeless camp.

She walked the streets of New York endlessly with just a few bits of change in her pocket. She stopped to grab a hot dog from a sidewalk vendor. "Miss, that will be 98 cents," he said.

Jamie reached in her pocket and pulled out 89 cents. She handed all her spare change to the vendor, smiled, and said, "That's all I have."

The vendor said, "Good enough, Lady." He noticed she was not well off.

While Jamie was preparing her hot dog with sauerkraut, relish and mustard, she looked up and saw an old office building. The words she read astounded her.

"Gamblers Anonymous"

The motto is "For all those in need. We are here for you."

"Gamblers!" Jamie thought to herself. "Am I a gambler?" While scarfing down her hot dog, she noticed that there were many people entering the building. Her body moved in a curious fashion toward the entrance of the old brick building.

She followed the people into this brick building. There was a spread of coffee and donuts on a table to the left. She helped herself until she was full.

"Ladies and Gentlemen, the meeting is about to begin," a voice hollered from a distance. Jamie followed the group of people into the room and took a seat in the back.

"Welcome to Gamblers Anonymous. My name is Bill and I'm a compulsive gambler." Many stories were told that evening. Jamie listened with all ears.

Then a lady stood at the podium. "My name is Jill and I'm a compulsive gambler."

The voices in the audience greeted Jill. "Hi, Jill."

"Hi, Everyone. Well, it's so nice to be here tonight. I have thirty days under my belt without making a bet." Applause from the group, then silence in the audience. Jill continued. "Thirty days. I never thought I could make it. If it weren't for you guys and my support group, I don't know what I would have done.

"I made my last bet in the stock market thirty days ago. Since then, it's been all uphill. I don't watch the stocks anymore. I don't worry about who's making money or who's losing money. I keep my nose to the grindstone. I know I'll never make the money back that I lost, but that's okay; I can sleep at night. I'm not obsessed with the market. I feel good now." Applause, applause from the group.

Jamie stood up and confronted Jill as she was leaving the podium. "Excuse me," she said.

"Yes, Dear?"

"Well, I'm new here; in fact, this is my first meeting. Jill, is the stock market really gambling? I mean, I never thought of it that way. Everyone plays from the age of eighteen years old on up. Is it really an addiction?" Jamie asked. "Isn't it just hard work? I mean, studying and learning the market, watching the trends. You know what I mean."

"Darling, the definition of a gambler is 'One who is out of control when they gamble everything, including what they have in their check-book or credit cards, any money they have or don't have. That includes borrowed money . . . until there is nothing left.'

"That's the definition of a compulsive gambler. Gambling is not limited to just playing games of chance, such as poker, twenty-one, slots, or craps. It's anything where you make a wager, small or large. A wager that may ruin your life, your work, and affect your husband or children.

"Gambling is a disease. A disease that can be kept under control by coming to regular meetings at Gamblers Anonymous. Gambling is a little bit different from all the rest of the addictions, such as alcohol or drugs. It's an emotional illness. You live for the emotional high, whereas alcohol or drugs is a physical illness.

"You get a high from gambling; you get a rush whenever you're in action or playing a game where money is involved. There are times you forget the world.

"All you want to do is stay in action. Play twenty-one or the stock market till eventually all your money is gone. And when it is you will find yourself sick inside, ashamed, not wanting to face the world.

"Sometimes you will find yourself homeless and ashamed to tell anyone your problem." Jill stared right into Jamie's eyes. "Then, of course, you will find yourself at Gamblers Anonymous. If you're one of the lucky ones."

Jill continued. "Let me tell you a secret. Gamblers gamble to lose, not to win. . . . For if they were winners they would have quit and walked away.

"But to a gambler there is never enough money in the world to win. The same is true of alcoholics. There's never enough booze in the world for them to drink; they drink till they pass out. A gambler gambles until there is nothing left."

Jill's long speech came to an end. She waited for a response from Jamie.

Jamie bowed her head in shame. "Thank you, Jill." She realized for the first time that she had a problem; she truly was in the right place: Gamblers Anonymous.

Jill invited Jamie to come up to the podium. "Why don't you tell us a little about yourself and how you got here."

Jamie tried to speak but she stuttered from fright,

"Hi, my name is Jamie. I need help." She broke down. Jill put her arms around her and took her into the ladies room.

Jamie had a good cry. "I had no idea I had a problem I thought I just had some bad luck. I never knew this could happen to me," she sobbed.

"Look at me. I had 150,000 dollars just about a month ago. Now I look in the mirror and I'm homeless. Look at my shoes; they've started to have holes in them. I haven't eaten anything decent in weeks." Jamie cried and cried on Jill's shoulder. "I have nowhere to go."

Jill handed her a tissue. "Jamie, let me help you. I have an apartment down the street. You can stay with me until you get on your feet. We can go to regular meetings and before long you will be fine, I promise," she said.

Jamie tried to smile. "Okay."

So Jamie stayed with Jill for well over a month. She listened and learned about what it was to be a gambler. The first thirty-days was rough for she had to come to terms with herself. She had to realize she had a problem. It was hard at times to realize that playing the stock market was gambling.

Over a period of time she came to terms with her disease of gambling. And Jill turned out to be her best friend. She was always there to help Jamie and give her the support she needed. They stayed up late every night discussing gambling and how Jamie could have developed this disease.

Within a month and a half, Jamie was ready. She found a new job as a secretary and was well on her way to recovery. She went to school part-time, studying to become a counselor. Her nights were filled with meetings and slowly but surely she was making her way back into the real world.

Jill asked Jamie one evening, "What drove you to seek help?"

"Jill, I was in the homeless compound for at least a month when a friend of mine, Amy, showed up with a book she wanted me to read. In fact, here's the book that changed my life. It's called 'Believe.' Jamie handed the book to Jill, who opened the book carefully.

"Believe"

It's time to stop doubting yourself, for you have so much to give, and so much that you deserve in return for your loving kindness.

Don't ever doubt what you give away to the world, for it will come back to you tenfold in time.

Know yourself and all your fine qualities. Life is for the living.

It's time to start fresh; it's time to start anew. Pretend that today is the first day of the rest of your life. It's time to start right now. It's time to believe. For if you believe, all great things will happen to you.

"That was beautiful," Jill said. As she handed the book back to Jamie, a tear rolled down her cheek.

Jamie smiled. "Jill, my gosh, oh my gosh! I'm supposed to return this book to someone in need. I have to go back to the homeless compound. I have to pass the book on," she said.

"Can I go with you?" Jill asked.

"Yes. Hurry! We got to go." They put on their coats and off they went to the homeless compound.

Jamie had already decided who she was going to pass the book on to Bobbie. He needed the book. He was in his wheelchair day in and day out. He could use some inspiration.

When they arrived at the homeless compound, there was Bobbie. Bobbie was different. He had his own apartment but spent his days at the homeless compound talking to all the new arrivals. They were his friends. Jamie stood right in front of Bobbie till he noticed her.

"Hey, Jamie, you look fine. How are you?"

"Fine, Bobbie, I've had a life altering experience."

"What kind of life-altering experience?" he asked.

"Bobbie, it's this book 'Believe.' It changed my life. I came here to pass this book on to you. You have to read it! It will change your life."

"Let me see the book." Jamie handed the book to Bobbie. As he opened the book "Believe," Jill and Jamie left the homeless compound slowly. . . .

"Believe"

Our lives are made up of so many special moments. We spend those special moments in different ways. Many times we spend those special moments in search of our true selves. Other moments are spent surviving day to day.

One day at a time. . . . We can experience each day anew, and with each new day comes a fresh new start. Living one day at a time allows us to truly enjoy life to its fullest. It's time to take another baby step. It's time to "Believe."

"Whoa!" He was taken aback. "Powerful stuff in this book." He thought and he thought. . . .

"Believe"

Believe in life and time will heal all wounds.

Chapter 6

"Believe"

Bobbie's life wasn't always depressing. Why, there was a time when his life was rich and full of promise. Bobbie grew up in Chicago. He ran his own travel company, mainly dealing with tours.

He was quite successful for the ripe young age of twenty-nine. He took advantage of most of his tour packages, for he would write about each and every new expedition for his tour magazine, which was distributed nationwide.

He was an avid skier. He loved to surf, hike and mountain climb. Bobbie was heavy into photography. One of his greatest expeditions was a photographic safari to Kenya, Africa. Some of his pictures were published in The National Geographic Magazine.

In the early eighties he decided to marry Kim. High upon a mountain top they exchanged their wedding vows. Bobbie had it all. The money was flowing in. Kim and Bobbie took regular trips together. Why one year it was Paris then Wales.

This year they decided to take a trip to Switzerland.

They wanted to ski the Alps. Bobbie brought along his photographic equipment, while Kim stayed by his side.

Skiing, as well as travel, was their life. On one bright and sunny day, high up on the Alps, they had all their gear in place and were ready for the first run of the day. Bobbie couldn't wait to take off; he loved to race.

"Com'on, Kim. I'll race you to the bottom," he said.

"You're on, Bobbie." Kim was quite a competitive skier herself. Off they went. Of course, Bobbie reached the bottom way before her. He smiled all the way down.

"Well, Kim, are you ready for another run?" He looked back at her and smiled.

Kim answered, "I'll catch up. Why don't you go ahead of me. I need to adjust my ski boots."

"Okay, Babe, see you at the lodge." With poles in hand off he went at a speed that was incredible. Faster and faster, he drove his muscular body to the limit. Bobbie was an adrenaline junkie, racing to the limits.

Suddenly he found himself out of control. He was headed right into a tree. He braced himself. He tried to avoid the tree, but he couldn't make his skis or body turn. The crash was inevitable.

He lay in perfect stillness, unable to get up. Within moments he was surrounded by the ski patrol. His body lay motionless on a stretcher. An ambulance was called. There were crowds around him.

Kim looked at her watch. She wondered what was taking Bobbie so long to ski back to the lodge.

A young man approached her. "Hey, Lady, did you hear about the skiing accident?" he said.

"What accident?"

"A skier was racing downhill and he crashed into a tree," the young man replied.

Kim had a funny feeling it was Bobbie. In fact, she knew it was Bobbie. "Is the young man alive?"

"He's breathing, but I think his body is in a million pieces. "Lady, look! Here comes the stretcher now. Let's go see." He motioned for Kim to follow.

Kim made her way through the crowd of people.

"Lady, stand back!" the paramedics shouted. "We have to get this guy to the hospital."

"Wait! Oh, my god, it's my husband."

They put an oxygen mask over his face. Bobbie was semiconscious. "Lady, you can come with us while we take him to the hospital." The sirens were blaring.

Kim waited at the hospital for several hours before they would give her any word. The next thing she knew the doctor told her they had to rush Bobbie into surgery. She waited patiently and prayed the whole time.

A whole day passed. The doctor asked for Kim to follow him into his office.

Kim asked anxiously, "Doc, is he going to be all right?"

The doctor spoke with a slight German accent. "I don't know how to tell you this. Your husband's accident was very severe. I'm surprised he's still alive."

Kim interrupted. "He's going to be all right?" Her raised voice revealed her concern.

The doctor blurted out the dreaded news. "He's paralyzed from the waist down. I don't know if he'll ever walk again. I'm sorry."

"Paralyzed! Can't we do therapy? Isn't there a chance he could walk again?" Kim broke; the tears rushed down her face.

"I don't think so. He hit that tree pretty hard. I mean, thank God his body turned and he hit the tree with his hip and not with his head. You know what I mean. If he had hit the tree full force with his head, he would be dead right now. He's pretty lucky just to be alive. It will take months of therapy just to get him to sit in a wheelchair. I'm so sorry," he said caringly.

"When can I see him?"

"Give it till tomorrow. We need to run more tests."

Kim was in shock. Early the next day, she was at the hospital. The nurses led her into Bobbie's ICU room. He was barely conscious. She sat down beside her husband and reached for his hand. Bobbie squeezed her hand gently, as if to acknowledge she was there. Tears rolled down her cheeks; she could barely contain herself.

The nurse explained to Kim that Bobbie was heavily sedated.

Several days passed. Bobbie seemed to be responding now. He recognized Kim.

"Bobbie, I love you. We'll make it through this." She lay her head upon his chest and forced a smile.

Bobbie seemed positive. He was brave. "Piece of cake Kim. They tell me I'll never walk again. I'll just have to show them, I guess. I'll walk again. I know I will." Bobbie had a tear in his eye.

"You will, Bobbie. And I will be there at your side. Don't worry."

Weeks went by; therapy had begun. Bobbie was getting stronger and stronger. Every part of his body was strengthening. But he was confined to a wheelchair. He was paralyzed from the waist down.

It was time for Bobbie to be moved out of the hospital; he had to go back to the States. He spent months and months with private doctors and therapists but they all said the same thing. "Sorry, you'll never walk again."

Over the months Kim stayed by his side. Bobbie's once positive attitude was dwindling. He had tried so hard to believe he would walk again, yet reality set in: he would be confined to a wheelchair for the rest of his days. He had several operations to fuse his disks together, but nothing seemed to help. He was in more pain now and took several pain pills a day. And when the pain got unbearable, he was given small doses of morphine.

This was rough on Kim. She watched this once-spirited man, whom she loved with all her heart and soul, deteriorate day by day. His spirit was down to nothing and all that was left was an angry soul.

Every day he yelled and screamed, "Why is this happening to me? I don't deserve this!"

Kim knew that most of the time it was the drugs talking. She didn't know how much longer she could hold on. With each day that passed, Bobbie's will was weakening; there were times he didn't want to live anymore. Kim didn't know how to help him. She didn't know what to do.

They decided to sell his business since Bobbie had no desire to work anymore. He was obsessed with going to therapy with hopes there might be a cure.

Kim found a job close to home so she could take care of Bobbie. Kim became the enabler. She took care of Bobbie's every whim. She covered for him when he had his fits of temperament. She turned her back when he took enormous amounts of morphine. She pretended that their life was just fine. Kim was the nurturer and caretaker. She refused to let Bobbie fall.

Bobbie had to learn to cope with society in his own way. He needed to understand how this new system in life worked. Kim did not help matters.

Why, if someone is always there to catch you when you fall, then how will you learn your lessons in life? This was Bobbie's lesson.

Life had always been so easy for him. No matter what he did in life he always was a success. Now it was time for him to take the fall and roll with the punches. Bobbie realized if he was going to get any better mentally, he had to let go of Kim. This wasn't an easy task for he knew she would never leave him willingly. In his heart he loved her very much. But Kim needed to learn her lessons as well. She needed to learn to let Bobbie fall.

One evening when Kim came home from work, Bobbie started screaming and throwing things. "Kim!" he shouted. "I can't take this anymore. I see the look on your face; it's as if you pity me. I'm half a man. We can never make love. I want you to get out of my life. I never want to see you again."

"Bobbie, what are you saying? I love you. It doesn't matter if we make love. I love you," she said.

"Kim, you'll never understand. I want you out of my life. I love you enough to let you go. I don't need your pity. There's the door. Get out!" he screamed. This was the only way Bobbie knew how to handle the situation.

Kim couldn't believe he was demanding she leave. She quickly gathered whatever clothes she could and made a hasty exit, slamming the door on the way out. She cried for months on end.

Bobbie's decision had been made. He did it for her own good. She needed a whole life and a whole man, not half a man. He drifted off into a deep sleep after shooting himself up with morphine.

Kim stayed away. She got her own apartment. It took time for her to realize that maybe, just maybe, Bobbie was right. She needed to work on herself; she needed a fresh start and a new life.

Day in and day out it was always the same. Bobbie stared out of the window from his apartment. The days turned into weeks, weeks turned into months, months turned into well over a year.

Bobbie wasn't getting any better mentally. He called upon the state department to collect disability checks. He had medical coverage but he no longer had a life. The only friends he had were the homeless. Day in and day out he hung around a select few to actively converse with.

Bobbie realized the homeless were not there because they wanted to be. He realized they were there because they had no choice or chance in life. Why, for example, there was Jed, who was quite smart. Jed had been at the homeless camp for at least two years. He ended up there due to a fire breaking out in his home. He had no known relatives to speak of and no one really wanted him. Jed was not incapable of mingling with the public; He'd rather live his life as a hermit.

Bobbie began a study of the homeless people. He felt most comfortable with them. He realized under most circumstances these people were outcasts like himself. They were people that nobody wanted. Yes, some had drinking problems; several of them were mentally ill. The majority of these people suffered from malnutrition and poor diet. Given the right medication, they could have survived in the real world.

Bobbie wanted to change his life so desperately. He finally took out his book "Believe" and read the words intently for guidance.

"Believe"

It's time to believe in yourself. There will be many days when you try to get up in the morning that things just don't go quite right. In fact, they may not go the way you would have hoped them to go.

There will be times when you have to talk to yourself and tell yourself things will get better.

There will be many times when people disappoint you and let you down. But those are the special times when you must pull yourself together. Trust your own judgment. Keep your life focused on believing in yourself and your inner strength.

There will be times when you feel physically challenged. It may be hard to face the world. Stay focused.

It will be just a matter of time before the light of knowledge will shine through.

Answers will be given and the light of the path will be shown to you.

You can be an inspiration to others. It may not be easy at times, but as you struggle you will find a much stronger sense of who you are Everything in life happens for a reason.

For life is a long journey through time, filled with so many choices. So when your days are filled with pain and longing and unexpected frustration just remember that the new challenges you face in life will help you to find the dreams that once were lost in the deepest part of your soul. Those dreams can resurface and come alive once more. And all you have to do is "Believe."

Those very words that Bobbie read touched the very heart of his being. He started to think and think. He searched his soul for the answers. "The homeless!" he thought. The answer was right there before his eyes.

He now had a quest. If he could help the homeless somehow, then all his suffering would not have been in vain. It was time for him to go home, for he had a lot of thinking to do. "I have to find a way to help them." He tossed in bed night after night. "There must be a way."

He opened his book once more, as if he were looking for just the right answer.

"Believe"

True gifts of the spirit. The gift of touching someone. What a beautiful gift this is. To be able to reach out and touch someone, not only physically, but on other levels.

With touching comes feelings, communication and love. What a beautiful gift to give someone in life. To be able to speak words for those who cannot. To say what is in each and every man's heart. To speak the right words at the right time for those less fortunate than us.

Learn to speak and feel with your heart. Let the words come from the deepest part of your very soul . . . "Believe."

Bobbie closed his book and knew what he had to do.

Why, it was so simple; the words he read made sense. He sat down on his computer and started researching agencies that would help the homeless. He worked day and night. He made phone call after phone call, pleading and asking for donations.

His friends in the homeless camp weren't capable of asking for anything. He would be their voice. Before too long things started falling into place. He was able to find housing for some. The ones who were able did handy work for their keep. He had doctors donate their time once a week. Medical students came to the homeless camp and gained invaluable experience ministering aid to the homeless.

Bobbie called storage companies to find out if they would spare storage spaces for the canned goods and blankets that were donated. Months passed and it was all coming together. He felt good. He felt needed.

Bobbie devised a check list system for each homeless person. He helped them fill out a brief questionnaire, for most of the Homeless could not read. Depending on their need Bobbie would go home and enter the information in his computer.

He would work 18 hours a day to help these people that were less fortunate than him. For the first time in a long time Bobbie felt at home helping the Homeless.

Maybe Bobbie couldn't walk, but he sure could talk. Before long he had counselors coming to speak with the homeless. He had people dropping off clothes and warm jackets for them, and to top it off, a donation was given on behalf of Bobbie for the homeless for a huge storage place in New York City. There were many beds that were provided for the homeless to sleep in.

His next task would be a huge one. He contacted Hugh Lomax's staff and proposed an idea. Hugh was so great at obtaining millions of dollars for starving children in other countries. Why not start a secondary cause of donations to help the homeless right here in the United States? Bobbies idea was explained to Hugh. Bobbie proposed that in each city there would be built a place for the people nobody wanted. A place that would have ample medical supplies, food, compassion and love. A place no one would shun. Hugh's people thought it was an excellent idea and great for hugh's publicity worldwide. They would pass the idea on to the right people and get back to Bobbie.

For the first time a realization hit him. He knew now why he was meant to have this horrible accident, for if this accident never would have happened, he would have never looked twice at the homeless.

Bobbie gained so much respect from the homeless camp. He finally felt important. He even used his skills as a photographer. He would photograph the homeless working hard storing can goods then, he would put those photographs on the internet and transmit them around the world for donations. His attorney upon request set up a nonprofit organization for the needy and the abused.

Bobbies life was so full. He didn't have time for anything but this quest. He put the homeless to work on the phones, teaching them as well, how to make Xerox copies and how to fax material. Never in history had so much been done to help the homeless.

One day out of the blue he received a phone call. "Hi Bobbie, it's me Kim." She spoke timidly.

There was silence momentarily. "Kim, hi how are you?" Bobbies voice projected a happy tone.

"I'm fine Bobbie, I just wanted to see how you were doing," she said.

"Kim do you have time to come over to my place for a little while? I want to show you something."

"I'll be right over."

When Kim arrived at Bobbies apartment he was so happy to see her. From beginning to end Bobbie explained everything to Kim. He even apologized to her. "Kim, my whole life was shattered after my accident. You were there for me; you were there for my every need. I truly loved you with all my heart and soul. But I had to let you go. You needed a life. I couldn't allow you to enable me. I wanted you to be happy." He smiled. "Are you happy?" he asked.

"Bobbie from what I've seen here I'm so happy for you. I want us to remain friends. If there's anything I can do for you in your quest, you can always count on me, she said proudly.

Kim let her feelings out. "You see Bobbie, after we broke up I was devastated. I spent many months in a shrinks office. I learned about co-dependency. I learned I wasn't helping you. Several co-dependency books later, I realized you were being kind to me by setting me free. This is the first time I was able to face you in months. And I must admit I had an ulterior motive. I came here so you would sign these divorce papers. I expected you to be all drugged up on morphine. I didn't expect this wonderful surprise you have shown me. I'm so happy for you Bobbie."

Bobbie took the divorce papers and while he was bending down and signing them, he told Kim the truth. "I'll sign these, there long over due. Just remember Kim we will always be friends." There was a twinge of hesitation on his part.

"Kim, I haven't touched drugs in months. I've been so preoccupied with my work." He smiled. "I have such a long way to go. I've only touched the surface of what wonderful miracles could be. Kim, the funny thing was, after you left I was at my lowest point in life. I was either going to kill myself, or I was going to make it." His eyes were focused on Kim.

"What made you want to live? she asked.

"Well, Jamie, gave me this book called 'Believe'. . ." Bobbie picked up the book and handed it to Kim. "I swear

Kim, the book helped me to change my life. It truly was a miracle. Here just open the book to a page. It has an answer for you."

Kim opened the book "Believe" and read aloud.

"*Believe*"

There comes a time in your life when we must exam our beliefs. Put them to a test. Belief allows you to open doors. Belief allows you to open minds and keep them open. Belief allows you to open your heart and never, never, close your heart again. It's time to open the door. It's time to walk through. For a new chapter in life is about to begin. "Believe". . . Pass it on. . . .

"Whoa! Bobbie, I'm taken aback. This is powerful stuff." she said.

"Kim! I forgot. I have to pass this book on. That's one of the rules."

"Well my friend I'll be glad to help you. Have an idea of who you want to give this to?"

"Yes. There's a new girl that just came into the camp. Her name is Linda. I know she can use this book. She's quite young. If anyone deserves a chance in life she does. Com'on we have to find her." Bobbie and Kim went to the homeless camp to find Linda. She was standing in line to get some food when Bobbie approached her.

"Hey, Linda, my name is Bobbie and this is Kim. Can I be of assistance to you?"

Linda wiped the tears from her eyes. She was shaking, for she hadn't eaten in days. She glanced down at Bobbie sitting in his wheelchair. "I heard about you," she said. "I heard how you helped so many. Maybe you can help me? I have nowhere to go."

"Linda. I've heard. I have something for you." Bobbie reached in the side pocket of his wheelchair and handed her the book "Believe." "Here take this book. Please open it," he pleaded nicely.

"A book. How can this help me?" she asked.

"Look! At me Linda; I'm living proof. It's a start! So take my advice and open the book. Go ahead! Open it anywhere. The truth shall set you free Darling."

Linda sat down and opened the book "Believe." She read the words out loud so Bobbie and Kim could hear.

"Believe"

Don't give up on life. Don't be concerned with finding the easiest way to travel. Follow your heart which will lead you to the person you really want to be.

Search for your truth and you will find your way. It's never to late to start again. For in the deepest part of your soul your search has just begun. If only you "Believe"

Linda sighed. The words she read aloud gave her comfort.

"Bobbie. Thank you. Can I share something with you. I'd like to tell you how I ended up here. My story is long. And I desperately need someone to talk to. Do you have the time?"

"I have all the time in the world." Bobbie sat in his Wheel Chair while she spoke. I won't say a word. I'll Just listen.

Kim left the two of them alone. She whispered into Bobbie's ear, then exited the picture.

"*Believe*"

Just one day could make a difference if you believe.

Chapter 7

"Believe"

So this is Linda's story as it was told to Bobbie.

Well, Bobbie, I was only twenty years old when I ran away from home. The arguments and fights in my family were too much for me to handle. Besides, within two months I'd be of legal age. I was always told I was a beautiful girl. I was blessed with jet-black shoulder-length hair, blue-green eyes and a slender figure.

I dropped out of high school, for there was too much arguing in the family for me to concentrate on my school work. Besides, I always wanted to be a hair dresser. But I would find a way to make it on my own. I was tough on the inside, and I would do whatever it took to make it financially. I always loved money; that was my downfall.

I was born and raised in Seattle and always had a burning desire to see the Big City. I had saved enough money from babysitting and house sitting to get a bus ticket to New York.

I figured when I got to New York I would find a job, and I would stay at the YWCA till I got on my feet. Anything was better than living in a home with no love. I refused to grow up and be like my parents. I never understood why they stayed married anyway.

Well, the Greyhound Bus stopped in the very heart of New York City. When the bus door opened the first thing I heard was the loud noise of the city. Then the hustle and bustle, horns honking and people walking at such a fast pace. Surprisingly, this excited the hell out of me. It was so different from the way I grew up.

So I checked myself into the YWCA, dropped off my luggage and out the door I flew to go job hunting. I got a job as a waitress in a local deli almost immediately. Being a waitress would only be a temporary job for me. I had much higher hopes for myself.

After several weeks on the job, I noticed a group of people that came into the deli almost every evening. What I noticed most was they seemed to be decked out in solid gold dripping from their hands and necks.

There always seemed to be two beautiful girls with this one guy. The reason that I noticed them was they were very loud and flamboyant.

It was my turn to wait on them. I hesitated but walked confidently toward their table.

"Hi, my name is Linda. I'll be your waitress. May I take your order?"

The young man spoke. "Yes, Darling. We'll have three

hot pastrami sandwiches, some chicken soup, and three dark beers."

The young man looked up and spoke to me in a softer tone. "Say! What's a pretty girl like you doing working in a place like this? It seems to me that you have a lot more going for you than working here."

"What do you guys do for a living?" I asked. "I'm always looking to better myself," I said cautiously.

"Well, the young girls work across the street at the Club Passion. They're exotic dancers." The girls giggled. "I'm what you might call their manager. I manage their money. I also manage their life." The girls giggled again.

"Why don't you come over one evening on your night off. I'll show you around. There's plenty of money in this line of work. By the way, my name is Billy. This here is Sandie and Brandie."

The ditsy girls in unison said, "Pleased to meet you."

Billy handed me his card. "Drop by any time, Sweets. I'll show you around the place; we run a high-class show. Someone as pretty as you deserves a lot more than this, Darling," he said.

I blushed. "Thank you. I'll think about it, Billy. Maybe I'll drop by in the next evening or so." I put his card into my uniform pocket.

When Billy and the girls left he made sure he left a sizable tip for me.

That evening I couldn't sleep. I was taken in by all that jewelry and flash the girls were wearing. I thought out loud to myself, "Exotic dancer . . . that might not be so bad. I could do that for a few months, make enough money to put myself through beauty school and the rest would be history." I had a plan.

The next evening, I was off from work. I dolled myself up in my best fitted, sleazy black dress. I bought a pair of rhinestone earrings and I was ready to rock and roll. So I made my way across the street to Club Passion.

The doorman asked me if he could help me. "Yes, please." I handed Billy's card to him.

"Wait here, Young Miss," he said.

Within moments, Billy greeted me at the door. "Well, hello there. If I remember correctly, your name is Linda!"

"Yes."

"Follow me; I'll show you around." Billy held his arm out for me to hold on to.

The music was loud in the nightclub. I noticed there was a long runway for the exotic dancers. As I watched, they danced suggestively to music, while stripping slowly down to their bare essence.

I also noticed a beautiful young girl stripping and flirting with a male customer. He padded her panties with a $100 dollar bill. She bent down and kissed the guy on his fat head. My eyes widened.

Billy looked at me and asked, "Do you want to dance for us?" He could tell that I was more than interested.

"We have strict rules at Club Passion," he said. "The men are not allowed to touch the women. Why, you can make up to 500 dollars per dance We have private booths where you can dance privately. We have bouncers if there is any trouble along the way, we're on it. You will be protected at all times.

"You dance every night for about four hours. We have choreographers that will help you map out your routine. Prostitution is not allowed here.

"However, whatever you do on your own time is up to you. The house's cut is 50 percent of whatever you make. It's that simple. And Linda, we provide the utmost protection. I can manage your money for you like I do for the others. I'll give you a good return on your money. I'll invest it for you, so in time you won't ever have to work."

He paused and took a breath from his long speech.

"You've seen how well off they are. I'll make sure you never want for anything! Well, what do you think?" He looked into my eyes.

I excitedly replied, "When do I start?"

"Meet me here tomorrow afternoon at 3 o'clock. I will connect you with all the right people and we will get you all fixed up. Within a week or so you will be dancing. I promise."

So I hung out with Billy at the bar and joked for several hours. I thought, "What an easy way to make a living."

The next day I gave my notice at work and was ready to be transformed.

It was 3 o'clock sharp when I arrived at the club. Billy was there to greet me. "Hey, Kid, you made it. I'd like to introduce you to Tommy."

"Hi, Tommy," I said.

He nodded.

"Tommy will be your personal valet. He, will show you the ropes and cater to your every whim." Billy smiled.

Several weeks passed. Tommy worked with me endlessly. He tried several new routines to see which best suited me. I had a natural ability for dancing. And Tommy told me that I had a great figure and loved to show off my body. I must admit I loved men to admire me. Billy told me I would be a natural at this job. And he was right.

Tommy told Billy that I'd be ready within a week. So I worked very hard on my routines. Well, I finally had put it all together. I had several costumes to pick from but I wanted to surprise Billy. So Tommy and I kept everything under wraps till opening night.

For some unknown reason I was more than confident. My grand debut would arrive tomorrow night. I couldn't sleep all night. I tossed and turned. All I kept thinking about was the enormous amount of money I would make.

Flashes of Sandie and Brandie were running through my head. Why, Sandie wore a three-carat diamond ring, and Brandie wore a tennis bracelet that could blind your eyes. But tomorrow night. . . . "Yes, it would be my turn."

The announcer spoke: "And now, Ladies and Gentlemen, Club Passion proudly presents . . . Miss Linda Day. . . ." The music escalated. "Let's have a round of applause for our newest kitten." Now the spotlight was on me!

Tommy said I was gorgeous. I wore a stunning cat outfit. I tantalized the men with my furry cat mask. Then I purred. I danced and danced and with each move I was sexy and suggestive. The men went wild.

Billy stood in the back of the room watching. He was salivating. He knew I was attractive, but the cat outfit made me even more alluring. He watched my every move. I dipped down low and exposed my body as if I were toying with each and every man.

A customer gave me my first 20 dollar bill. So I let him place the bill in between my legs and my leopard skin bikini. The men in the audience yelled and cheered for me to come over to them. They were all lined up.

Each man had a different amount of money to give to me. And I was loving every minute of it.

When I was through dancing, Billy asked me to step into his office. I followed.

He said, "Linda, Girl, you were good. I mean you were really good. Are you sure this is your first time dancing?"

I answered, "Yes, Billy. At home I used to dance at regular nightclubs all the time, but nothing like this, I swear."

"Well, Girl, you are a natural. How much money did you make?"

I reached into my panties and took out several $20 bills.

"Let's see." I handed the money to Billy; he counted it for me.

"Not bad for your first night, 300 dollars. I get half and you get the rest. Not bad; 150 dollars is your cut. Well, what do you think?"

"I think this is wonderful. I can't believe it. Billy, it was so easy."

"Well, Linda, why don't you run along home and we'll see you tomorrow."

"Okay, Billy, see you tomorrow." I couldn't wait. Soon I'd be able to afford my own apartment in the Upper East Side of Manhattan.

Weeks went by and I danced almost every night. Before month's end, I had saved well over $3000.

So I called for a meeting with Billy. We met the next day in a coffee house nearby.

I told Billy I had enough money to get my own apartment. I asked, "Will you help me?"

"What do you have in mind, Girl?"

"Well, I want to live in the Upper East Side."

Billy said to me, "Linda, why don't you let me hold on to your money. Walking around the streets of New York with that amount of money is just plain crazy. Besides, I like my girls to only have about 100 dollars in their pocket. I mean, you never know what's going to happen in this city.

"I do know of an apartment on The East Side. In fact, it's the same apartment building that Sandie and Brandie live in. Do you want to see it tomorrow?" he asked.

"Yes."

"Meet me at noon at this address."

Billy handed me the address while I handed him my money.

"See ya tomorrow, Babe," he said.

Bright and early the next morning I was ready to go. I met Billy at the apartment building at noon sharp. He showed me around the building. The one-bedroom apartment had a view of most of New York. There was a gym in the building and a doorman. The apartment was first class all the way and furnished to boot. I just loved it. The rent was steep; it was $1800 per month. But I knew I could make the money dancing. So I took the apartment.

And I thanked Billy for helping me. Billy mentioned that he would take care of me. I would have fine jewelry, the best of everything. I couldn't pass up a deal like this. As long as I had $100 in my pocket I was fine. I thought Billy was right. And, besides, he promised to invest some of my money as well.

As the months passed I made excellent money dancing. My next great feat was to have Billy buy me a brand new BMW. I couldn't wait. Billy explained for insurance purposes he would keep the car registration in his name.

So my car was paid for and I had a brand new apartment. I really wanted jewelry just like Sandie and Brandie. Billy bought me everything I wanted. He treated me real fine.

He would take us ladies out several times a week to other nightclubs just to show us off. The three of us were inseparable. I was living the life I had always dreamed of.

You know, I don't exactly know where things started to get bad, but they did.

I had worked very hard at my job with the hopes of someday owning my own hair salon. It seemed the harder I worked the less I had to show for it. I mean, I had a lot of things; Billy was so good to me in the beginning.

I became best friends with Sandie and Brandie. We shopped together; we did everything together.

I remember one evening I was hanging out at Sandie and Brandies's apartment. We were drinking and getting smashed. The doorbell rang and, sure enough, it was Billy. We were glad to see him.

Billy sat down and had a few drinks with us. We turned the music up loud. Brandie was dancing with Billy, and before I knew it they disappeared into her bedroom. I was left talking to Sandie. "What's up with that?" I asked.

Sandie said, "Just close your eyes, Girl; it happens all the time." About an hour passed before Brandie and Billy emerged. Brandie sat down and talked to me like nothing had happened. The next thing I knew Sandie went into the bedroom with Billy and they were getting it on. I couldn't believe it. About an hour later Sandie emerged and sat next to me on the couch, just like nothing happened.

Billy motioned for me to come into the bedroom. He said he wanted to talk to me. I was hesitant. The girls told me to go if I wanted to keep my job. So against my better judgment I went into the bedroom. The conversation went as follows:

"Linda, you are really beautiful. Come here, Babe." Billy drew me closer to him. He ran his hands down my breasts. He kissed me with deep passion. He was undressing me when I pulled away abruptly. "Hey, what's-a-matter, Babe? I want you," he said. "Don't pull away from me."

"Billy, I can't do this, do you understand?" I shouted. I broke away from his slobbering all over me and ran as fast as I could out of the bedroom. I kept on running till I reached my own apartment. I was shaking. I didn't know what the repercussions would be over this. But I wasn't a hooker. I had no desire to go to bed with Billy. He was my boss. I just didn't get it. First he had Sandie, then he had Brandie, then he wanted me.

The next evening I went to work as usual and put in a full shift. After work Billy motioned for me to come to the bar. I did. "Linda, I don't get it. Why did you embarrass me and push me away, Girl. What's wrong with a little sex? Sandie and Brandie and I have been getting it on for a long time now. I thought you would love to join in.

"Girl, you really humiliated me in front of the girls. I won't put up with that. If it weren't for me you'd be a two-bit waitress down the street. I made you. And I own you. You can at least have the decency to treat me a little nicer." Billy grabbed my arm. "Do you understand?" he snarled.

I was scared of losing everything I had. So I gave in. "You're right, Billy," I said. "Why don't we try again."

Billy smiled. "That's my girl. Let's have a few drinks and we can go to your apartment for a while." I nodded.

Well, Billy and I got it on. We had sex every night for months. Surprisingly, it wasn't all that bad. I became his main lady. Billy was always buying me things. All I had to do was say, "Gee, I really like that," and it was mine.

I was getting used to this lifestyle. Then one evening Billy asked me to come up to his apartment. I was excited. This was the first time I was invited there.

He had a gorgeous place on Park Avenue. That evening

was special We had a candlelight dinner in the living room. Billy's apartment had wall-to-wall picture windows. We had a view of all of New York City.

Billy told me he had a friend coming up to the apartment. The guy's name was Jim. He told me that Jim was one of the investors in the club. He had poured a lot of money into Club Passion. He said. Jim had seen me dance on several occasions and found me very attractive. He wanted to meet me. At first I was flattered. Then Billy explained that Jim wanted to go to bed with me.

"No, Billy, I can't do that!" I said.

"Linda, just this one time, Babe. Jim is one of our major investors. I can't say no to him, Girl. We could all lose our jobs. Please, just this once," he pleaded.

The thought of this made me sick. I didn't know what to do. I was now a high-paid call girl. I hated the thought of it. The doorbell rang. It was Jim. Billy introduced me to him. We had some small talk and a lot of booze. Billy told me he had to go to the store and get some smokes.

Shortly thereafter Billy left the apartment and Jim sat really close to me. He started kissing me all over. He pulled my panties down. Then he ravaged me.

It was all over so quickly. Within an hour Billy was back. We all chatted for a while as if nothing happened. Jim told Billy he had to go. We walked him to the door. He kissed me good night. Billy never asked what happened.

He joked with me the rest of the evening. I asked Billy if he could take me home. I was tired. And he did.

When I got into my apartment, I took a long hot shower just to rinse the stink off of me. I hated Billy and what he did to me. I knew this was just the beginning. There was no way out. I would be passed on from man to man. I needed time to think. I remember I cried myself to sleep.

I didn't sleep well. In fact, I was so sick inside I couldn't make my shift. I thought to myself, "What have I become?" Was it so important to have all these material things? I didn't even have a bank account. Why, everything was in Billy's name. I knew in my heart what I must do.

The phone rang. It was Billy. "Hey, Linda, what's up, Girl? Why aren't you working?" he asked.

"Billy, I think I'm coming down with something. Maybe it's the flu."

"I'll be right over," he said.

"Oh, my god, he's coming here." I didn't know what to do or how to handle this situation. Within moments the doorbell rang. I opened the door and let Billy in.

"I think we have to talk, Linda."

I nodded.

"Look, I'll be very diplomatic about this. I know why you're sick. It's because I asked you to go to bed with Jim isn't it?"

I nodded again.

"Linda, that was a rare occasion. He's an investor. And any time an investor wants one of our girls, we can't say no. I was put in a position. Don't you understand? I can't promise it won't happen again. But I can ward him off onto some other girl. Now come here, Babe; let me hold you," he said.

"Billy, I've been doing a lot of thinking. I don't want to be anyone's hooker. Do you understand? That is not part of my job. I'm a dancer. I don't have to go to bed with every Tom, Dick and Harry. And I'm not going to anymore."

"Bravo, Little Angel!" Billy clapped his hands. "So what do you plan on doing about this?" he asked.

"Well, I have enough money saved. I can get out now and buy myself my hairdressing business. I don't have to put up with this."

"With what money?" he asked.

"What do you mean . . . what money? The money I've been giving to you all this time." I was starting to panic.

He stood up and shouted, "Linda, if you walk now, you walk with just the clothes on your back!"

"What do you mean, Billy? That money is mine. You said you would just hold it for me and invest it."

"Linda, I did invest it. Sorry, the investment went bad, Darling. Sue me."

Now I really panicked. "My god! You mean to tell me if I don't do what you say, I have nothing?"

"You got it. You have nothing. So! If I were you, I would

think about this conversation tonight and let me know what you want to do in the morning." Billy raised his voice. There was a seriousness about him. He stood up and headed for the door.

"Just take a good look around here, Girl. You have it all. But you have nothing if you leave. . . . That's Nothing! Billy slammed the door.

So, Bobbie, I thought about it the next morning. I packed my things . . . what little I had . . . and I left the apartment with just the clothes on my back. I wandered the streets for several days debating if I should go back to him. But in my heart I knew I just couldn't do that. And that's how I ended up here with nothing."

Linda finished her story with a sigh and looked at Bobbie for his reaction.

Bobbie said, "Linda, you have something. You have your self respect. You learned a good lesson. Money isn't everything; it's what's inside that counts. You refused to prostitute yourself for Billy. In the end he would have owned you and your life."

Linda nodded with shame. "What am I going to do now, Bobbie? I have nowhere to go." She started crying uncontrollably.

Bobbie said softly, "Linda, take this book 'Believe.' Follow me, Girl. You can stay with me for a while till we figure things out. Okay?"

Linda smiled. There was an angelic look about Bobbie. Somehow she trusted him.

"Linda, do me a favor before we go," he said. "Just open the book 'Believe' to any page. We need some guidance here."

Linda opened the book.

"Believe"

Speak and you will be heard; let your words always be kind and you will be judged. For you will be watched from above. Remember, the angels always watch over the needy.

Give freely to all, and you shall receive so much more blessings in return. Listen to the troubles of others and your own problems shall slowly disappear.

Treat each day as your last, treasuring each sight and sound. Accept what you have. Don't make money your god. Strive with all your heart and soul to be greater than you were before.

Ask and even your smallest wish shall be granted. For all you have left is to "Believe."

Linda looked into Bobbie's eyes. There was warmth and compassion deep down inside. The book "Believe" gave her encouragement. So she followed Bobbie home, pushing him in his wheelchair all the way.

Over the months that passed, Linda became best friends with Bobbie. She learned his business inside out. Her desire to help the poor was overwhelming. Together they set up functions for donations for the homeless. Linda learned the computer and she worked the phones. She had a deep desire to help mankind. Her life had turned around, thanks to Bobbie and the book "Believe."

Bobbie had a surprise for Linda. One afternoon he handed Linda a certificate in an envelope. She opened it. It read: Admission To Norman Main Beauty School.

"Oh, my god, Bobbie. I can't believe you did this. Where did you get the money to pay for something like this? I can't accept this. It's way too much money to pay for my beauty school. I mean, it must have cost you well over 5,000 dollars." Linda sat in the chair, overwhelmed.

"Linda, I have an ulterior motive. I want you to go to beauty school on one condition," he said slyly.

She was all ears. "Yes, Bobbie?"

"The condition is you go to school and pass with flying colors, for this is your destiny and this is your dream. When you finish you can pay me back by donating free haircuts to the homeless for the tune of 5,000 dollars. And it doesn't matter how long it takes you to pay it back. You will be giving of your heart and your soul," he said.

Linda was so happy. She would pass beauty school within the year and get a job, and in her spare time she would be by Bobbie's side helping the homeless. And that's the way the story went.

The time came when Linda asked Bobbie, "Now that my life is on track, don't I have to pass this book on?"

"Yes, you do, Linda. If you want your life to stay on track you have to pass the book on." He smiled.

"Well, what are we waiting for? We'll have to go down to the homeless camp and pass it on." She grabbed Bobbie's wheelchair with excitement. "Let's go, Slowpoke."

"Okay! Linda, do you have any idea who you're going to pass the book on to?" he asked.

"No! Bobbie, can I wait till we get down there? I want to look around to see who needs the book the most."

"Sounds good to me." He smiled again.

They reached the homeless camp, where there were many people gathered around, especially in the food line. Bobbie had organized the homeless camp. He had volunteers around the clock. One of the volunteers grabbed Bobbie. "Hey, Bobbie, there's a man over there looking for you. He says he's heard a lot about you. He used to be part of the homeless camp and he wants to talk to you."

Bobbie wheeled his chair over to Joe. "I've heard you were looking for me. Can I help you? My name is Bobbie and this is Linda. Can I be of service?"

"Yes, you're just the person I wanted to see. I'm Joe. I

have a check for you and the homeless camp. Here's a donation. It's not much, but I know you can put it to good use. My life is going real well," Joe said.

Bobbie opened the envelope. The check was made out to his corporation for $5000 Bobbie showed it to Linda. "God sure works in mysterious ways. Thank you, Joe." He shook Joe's hand.

"Joe, Linda's life has been turned around as well. She wants to give the book 'Believe' away."

Joe smiled and asked, "Linda, have you decided who you want to give the book 'Believe' to?"

"Yes! That lady in the corner." Linda pointed to a shabby lady off in the distance.

Joe shouted, "That's Angie! By gosh, I haven't seen or heard from her in years. She always sat in the corner by herself. She doesn't bother with anyone. She sits by the fire huddled over while she eats and warms her frail hands. She's still wearing that same old, shabby gray outfit. I think it still has the same holes in it from when I left. I can't believe it!"

Bobbie called out, "Angie! Hey, Angie, come over here!"

Angie looked in the direction of the noise and saw Linda, Joe and Bobbie watching her. She made her way over to the group ever so slowly.

"I'm Angie. What can I do for you?"

"Here, Angie, I have this book I want to give you," Linda said.

Angie reached under her moth-eaten gray sweater and pulled out a pair of old reading glasses which she slowly put on. She held the book in her hand and read the title out loud. "Believe"

"What is this book anyway?" She examined the book carefully. 'Believe.' "Oh, com'on. You want me to read this book?" There was just a flicker of a smile on her face.

Joe, Linda and Bobbie all started talking to Angie at once. "Angie, trust us. It changed our lives. Just open the book to any page. The book has answers. It will change your life," they said in unison.

Angie stared deeply into their eyes. "You mean this book 'Believe' changed your lives? I always thought nothing could change your life but you." Angie tossed the book with passion into the dumpster.

Joe, Linda and Bobbie gasped with surprise.

Angie leaned forward and asked, "Do you have any idea who wrote this book?"

They looked blankly at one another for the answer. "We don't know."

One by one, Angie whispered into their ears. "I know." There was a long pause of silence.

They eagerly awaited her answer. Angie stood straight up, she was proud. Then she blurted out "I wrote the book with the help of my father." She stared deeply into their eyes.

"You. . . ! Wrote this book?" Joe mumbled.

She pointed her finger at herself. "You don't believe me, do you? You think I am deranged, old, loony. Well, I have a story to tell you." She shook her head while her eyes rolled up. "Cop a squat, Gang; take a load off. For the story I tell you is pure of heart."

All eyes were riveted on Angie as she spoke. Except for Joe's eyes. He raced over to the dumpster to try to retrieve the book "Believe."

Angie turned and watched Joe dive into the dumpster, trying to retrieve the book. "Hey, Joe!" she shouted. "Leave that book right where it is. That's where it belongs. Come back over here, Son. I have a story to tell."

Joe sat down reluctantly and listened.

"Believe"

Follow the spirit within your heart.

Chapter 8

"Believe"

And this is my story, as well as my father's story.

Black Thursday 1929. . . . It was Tuesday, October 29, When Wall Street's stock exchange experienced a wave of panic selling. So my father told me. An earlier sell-off on the previous Thursday, "Black Thursday, " combined with Tuesday's sales led to a collapse in stock prices and the loss of many Americans' fortunes.

My father was one of those Americans who lost his fortune. He told me this story over and over again as a child. Almost as if there was a panic within his voice each time he repeated the story to me. He remembered in detail men jumping to their death from office buildings. Others gathered in the streets outside the stock exchange to learn how much they had lost; Father was one of them.

My dad was the love of my life. I was his only child, for my mother died while she was giving birth to me. So all we had was each other. In those days Dad owned a small butcher shop in New York City. We always had food on the table. Dad had great dreams for us: he wanted us to have our own home; he wanted me to have a backyard to play in.

Dad virtually put almost all his money into the stock market, for just before the crash the economy was booming.

"Angie, the love of my life," he would say. "Soon you will have it all, Darling. I promise. I know you lost your mother, and I lost my wife; but the money I have invested for you, My Child, will make us rich beyond all our wildest dreams."

Now, mind you, I was only three years old at the time. None of this made too much sense to me until in later years. After the crash, the American economy was dead. Banks fell as people ran on them to withdraw their savings. (In those days the Federal Deposit Insurance was nonexistent.) A total of 16 billion dollars was lost, an astronomical sum in those days. Many hard working people lost all the money they had deposited into the banks.

Dad said fear had gripped the nation. Dad kept some money under his mattress, about $2000. That was a lot of money in those days. I think that's how we made it through the hard times.

Dad didn't stay in business too much longer after the crash, for on several occasions there was a run on many of the supermarkets and Dad feared for his life. He boarded up the butcher shop. He took me by the hand and we walked through the streets of New York. We waited in bread lines just like the rest of the people. Dad swore if he could find a way out of this mess we would never be poor again. He would find a way to help the poor.

Dad kept a journal through all the lean times. Dad was a very positive man. He didn't believe in handouts. But most of all he did "Believe..."

He believed that everything in life happens for a reason; and even though we were going through these hard times, we would be better off somewhere in time.

Dad told me years later that the best thing that ever happened to the country was when Franklin D. Roosevelt came into office in 1933. After his inauguration, Roosevelt's "first 100 days" changed history. But the recovery was very slow and took many years.

Dad said it wasn't until about 1937 that the economy was improving. In 1939, the country began to pull out of the depression. And so did my father. He had seen enough poverty in one lifetime for the memory to last for the rest of his days. He made sure that each and every day I would be reminded of the lean times; Dad never wanted me to forget.

My father never re-married. I thought at times he was quite lonely, but Dad would smile and say, "Angie, you're the light of my life. You bring so much joy into my life I hardly have room for another."

It wasn't until December 7, 1941, when the Japanese bombed Pearl Harbor, that our lives started to radically change. World War II was well underway and my father, being the smart man he was, decided to get involved. He decided to start small. He knew a lot about being a butcher and found a way of preserving meat in cans and shipping it off to our men overseas. What started out as a small business grew by leaps and bounds. "Canned Goods" for the military while they were in combat was how he made his living.

Dad started out in a very small warehouse. Within a year he had his own factory. He invested whatever money we had back into the factory. He was a proud man.

He employed many workers. The time Dad and I spent together grew few and far between. But the memories of him still linger on till this day.

As busy as he was, he always had time for me, especially at dinner. We would have quite a spread each night; and after dinner Dad would sit in his room, have a sip of brandy and write in his journal. I would sit along Dad's bedside and ask him what he was writing about.

He would comment: "My Child, this journal is for you. When I am long gone, the words that I write will be remembered. I write of love and strength and hope and belief. I write of the lean times of the depression, the poverty of the homeless, how man needlessly suffers without rhyme or reason. I write words of inspiration. I write to give each and every man in this world hope, not despair.

"But the time I spend writing, My Darling, is so little as of late, for my business is growing so fast." Dad paused.

"Lights out." He picked me up and tickled me. "Well, it's time for me to tuck you in, so let's get a move on," he jokingly said.

Before too long I hardly saw my father at all. His business was thriving, along with the war. I was growing up fast. I never knew what it was like to be poor. I always had what I needed. And Dad made sure I always had whatever I wanted.

There were many Sundays when Dad and I spent our time together. He now made it a point for us to be together each and every Sunday like clockwork. He was working so hard, but Sunday was our time to walk in the park and talk and have a picnic.

But one day I noticed something a little out of character for my dad. Dad wanted to spend a lot of time in our old neighborhood. He took me for a walk among the slums of New York where what once were pretty apartment buildings were now crack houses and the homeless wandered the streets. I was scared.

At one point I grabbed my dad's arm and held on to him for dear life.

"Don't be afraid, My Child," he said.

"Dad!" I cried "I want to go home! I don't want to be here!"

"Now, now, My Little Darling, I've brought you here to our old neighborhood so we can remember the lean times." He turned toward me.

"Angie, look at me! These people don't want to be here any more than you or I. You see, My Child, they have hit rock bottom. Their luck ran out, just like my luck ran out at one time. I don't ever want to forget that.

"This is a crude reminder of how times can change for all of us in a blink of an eye. When the stock market crashed in 1929, well, that's something I'll never forget. This is a good reminder of what could have been for you and me.

"But I never gave up. I believed there was more to life than what I saw here on the streets. I believed with all my heart and soul that I could make a difference, that I could change things. And that, My Darling, is the difference. I Believed. . . ."

I bent my head down and cried, as my dad comforted me.

Dad reached into his pocket and pulled out a twenty-dollar bill. He went up to a man who was sitting on the ground. The man was dressed in a gray sweat outfit with many holes in his shirt. His feet were bare and his clothes were tattered.

My dad went up to him and he handed the man a twenty-dollar bill. The man looked up. "Thank you," he said.

My father replied, "Believe. There is hope."

As we were walking to the car, my dad said to me, "Angie, with all my heart and soul, I want you to remember this day like no other. Most of all, I want you to share whatever wealth you may have in the future with the poor. Please, My Child, always remember..." A tear fell down his cheek.

My father was like no other. He had compassion and love and he cared for many. He gave away a lot of his money to the homeless. At times I thought he was a saint.

Years passed; I was growing up. I spent a lot of time helping in my dad's factory. I learned how to do office work and run the company with him.

Dad set up many charities for the poor over the years. My life was just as dedicated to helping mankind as was Dad's. I dated several men, but never found anyone as good as my father. I guess I measured every man I met to him. I know that wasn't right, but I never married.

I wanted everything in life to be so perfect. I never found the love of my life that I was looking for. I found love in different ways by watching my father. How he would hand out money to the poor. How he would work 80 hours a week while donating his time to try to make life better for the homeless.

My years were spent following in my father's foot steps. I knew of nothing else in life that would bring me joy and happiness than helping people less fortunate than myself. All that money could buy would never touch the dreams and hopes for a brighter tomorrow. I dedicated my life to his cause, now my cause.

It wasn't till later years that I took up photography and traveled the world. I went to Europe. I visited China. I spent a lot of time in India living with the Monks. I learned about spirit. I saw the poverty in India and Africa. I photographed the starving children. I photographed it all. I hung the photographs in every corner of my room as a hard core reminder that we all need to contribute to the world as a whole.

A lot of my photographs hang in museums. I donate most of the money to starving children in this country, for I learned a lesson in my travels. I learned what is most needed in life is to help your own people in whatever country you live in. Since I live in America, this is where I choose to help my people, no matter what race, creed or religion.

I also noticed while I traveled the world that so many people from America gave to other countries to support their poor. I saw people adopt children from different countries. Yet, who is helping our country?

I wondered why we have people walking the streets, why we have people living in San Francisco in a park. I photographed hundreds of homeless living in the Bay Area. What is so wrong with our country that we can't all donate just a little and form a charity that would wipe out poverty in America? If we all donate just one dollar per month, can you even imagine the dent that we would put into America as a whole?

I wanted to do so much for mankind. Through my photos, I could tell my story; my photographs would tell it all.

I was on my way back from India when I got word my father had taken ill. When I arrived in New York, I rushed as fast as I could to the hospital.

There he was, lying in a bed with oxygen. I cried. My god, what had happened? I felt so bad. I had been out of the country for so long that I wasn't able to give him the support he needed. I know he worked himself to death. I was in shock.

The doctor led me to his office and kindly said, "Angie, your father has had a major heart attack. His arteries are blocked, but he's too weak to be operated on. We need to wait a while to see how it goes."

"Is he going to make it?" I shook as I spoke those words.

"Angie, we don't know. We'll know in the next 48 hours. If he can pull though and gain strength, he'll make it. If not," the doc shook his head, "all we can do now is pray."

Over the next 48 hours, I never left my father's side. At times it seemed he was going to pull through. He held my hand and could speak very faintly.

"Angie, don't worry," he whispered. "I love you." Just remember I'll always love you. You've been my love, my spirit, my hope and the love of my life. When your mother died giving birth to you, you were special to me, so very special." There were tears in my father's eyes. I had to be brave. I held his hand and never let him go.

The next morning he seemed to be gaining a little strength. The doctors let him sit up. He had a second wind "Angie, you're still here. That's my girl. My briefcase is over there. Can you get it for me?" He motioned.

"Dad, please, no work. It's not important now. I want you to get better."

"Angie, please hand me my briefcase. I have something in there for you."

I did as he requested and I opened the briefcase. There was Dad's journal. It was a brown book and on the cover written in gold letters was the word "Believe." Dad reached into the briefcase and handed me the book.

"Angie, this book is yours." He half-smiled.

"Dad, why? I mean, you're getting better," I said.

"Listen to me, please. I don't have a lot of time left. Open the book anywhere to any page, and read the words to me," he implored.

I read the first page out loud to my father.

"Believe"

"This book is dedicated to my daughter Angie for all the times we shared together, for her undying dedication. This book is for you, Angie. This book is for the world to see. When I pass on, all there will be is this part of me, the part of me who loved life, the part of me in spirit that believed. So, my daughter, carry on my legacy, my life-long quest. Keep writing in the journal, for there will be so many new and wonderful journeys for you to tell."

I read on.

"Believe"

Angie, this life is the only one that we will remember in this lifetime. Never be discouraged in your efforts. Please replace your weaknesses with positives; take all the broken pieces in your life and replace them by recreating your dreams of mankind.

Never measure the future by what you did in your past; let yesterday become a memory and tomorrow be filled with new hope and new promises of helping mankind.

Angie, always help the poor and the homeless, lest you be poor one day yourself.

And most importantly, pass the book on to thousands.

If you help one person in mankind, Angie, you've helped a world full of souls.

Love Dad.

I closed the book gently and cried. My father motioned with his hands for me to come near. He was so weak now. I lowered my head so he could whisper in my ear. The words he softly spoke were . . . "I love you, Angie. Believe. . . ." That was the last breath that he took.

I paused to gather my thoughts. I kissed his cheek so softly while holding his hand and said, "I love you, too, Dad."

Over the years I added to my father's journal. What once were his words now became mine.

Angie paused and sighed. "And that's my story."

Joe, Linda and Bobbie were speechless.

Then Angie stood up from the cold cement and brushed herself off.

"Com'on, Guys, follow me. We have some work to do."

Off in the distance there was a gold Ford Mustang. Angie stopped at the car, reached into her pocket to get the car keys and opened the trunk. Inside of the trunk were several hundred copies of the book "Believe."

Everyone looked around at one another with amazement. The story was true.

Angie handed several copies of the book "Believe" to each of them.

"What do we do with the books, Angie?" they asked.

Angie started walking off, but she turned back slowly and said, "Pass them on! Pass them on to everyone in need. To the homeless. To the poor. To the Salvation Army. Let the world know there is hope. For all you have to do to turn your life around is 'Believe' Yes, 'Believe' it can happen, and it will. Just 'Believe' and you will make it happen. 'Believe. . . .' she whispered. As she walked off into the distance, her voice grew faint. "Believe, My Children, just Believe. . . ."

Angie had so much more work to do. She had an endless number of homeless camps to visit and many dumpsters to fill with books. She knew in her heart that if she were to hand these books out while dressed in fine clothes, very few would read or understand. Ah! But if they found these books in a dumpster or garbage can... What a treasure to be found!

The End

Pass This Book On To Someone In Need!

"Believe"

A writer's opinion; by Dayle Schear

Always know the answers lie within you. Just Believe with all your heart and soul.

When I began to write this book Believe, I was at an all-time emotional low in my life. The more I wrote, the more I began to Believe. My characters came alive; they were my friends.

I wrote through experience and from people I once met...People who touched my heart at one time. . . . People who touched my life. While I was writing this book, something very special happened: my life began to turn around. The more I believed; the more I manifested good in my life. I reached down to the bottom of my very soul for words that flowed from within my mind to the paper. Words that, when I wrote them, meant nothing until I read them.

And when I read these words, they had deep meaning for me in my life, as well as for the reader. I started to look at life in a different way.

Now, mind you, I've always felt deeply for the homeless and for the poor. But these words that I wrote connected me to my spirit. I knew then I had tapped into a very deep part of my soul that had been virtually untouched.

For now I have a quest, a burning desire to help those

that are less fortunate than us. I realized that we are not helpless. We can't turn the other cheek.

You know, when you pass a homeless person on the street...a man or woman who is broken in spirit and holding a sign that says "I will work for food..." how many times do you turn your head and pretend he doesn't exist?

We all want to be hero's in life, yet few have that chance. If each and every one of us donated but $1 to the homeless, can you even imagine what a great difference this could be? We spend millions on charity in other countries; well, maybe it's time we spend the money right here in our own backyard.

So scrounge up some blankets. Dig up some old clothes and shoes. Take a few items to the homeless. Smile when you see these homeless people, say a kind word give from your heart. For if each and every one of you look deep inside your closet and give away a warm blanket or a used coat. You to can make a difference.

This Book Is Magic: It Changes People's Lives

"Believe"

Every time someone purchases this book *"Believe,"* a portion will be donated to the homeless by me personally. My accounting will be set up in my foundation; through ESP & Me, a percentage of the net proceeds will be given to the homeless. It's not a lot, but it's a start. So follow in my footsteps and please. . . . Make a difference and give to the homeless.

About The Author

Psychic Dayle Schear was born in Newark, New Jersey, the youngest of two daughters; but soon Dayle's parents moved the family to Los Angeles.

While growing up in Los Angeles, Dayle more fully realized her Psychic potential when she randomly picked up a deck of Tarot cards. She studied the cards for ten years and devoted many years to giving free readings and helping people. She learned, over a period of time that most everything she told people had come true.

Inevitably, the world-famed Psychic, Peter Hurkos, discovered Dayle's talent. Following their encounter, she underwent six years of vigorous training with Peter until his death. Dayle is his "only living protege."

In 1988 Dayle married a local boy from the Hawaiian Islands, Blythe Arakawa. Together with their prize possessions, German shepherds, they divide their time between Honolulu, Hawaii and Lake Tahoe, Nevada.

Dayle is also the author of *Dare to be Different!*, which describes the eventful, spiritual journey of a Psychic. *The Psychic Within,* true Psychic stories. *Tarot for the Beginner* (Blue Dolphin, 1994, now in its third printing). Learn how to read the cards in one hour or less. Dayle has her own chapter in The Top 100 Psychics in America by Paulette Cooper. And soon to be released: *What If?* a spiritual journey into one's mind.

Dayle lectures throughout the United States on E.S.P. She had an on-going television talk show called "ESP & You" on a Honolulu CBS affiliate for fourteen years. Now you can find Dayle's show on KITV 4, ABC Honolulu. In her spare time, she is a guest on numerous National Television talk shows as well as radio talk shows throughout the nation.

She has worked for U.S. Navy intelligence in Hawaii and with law enforcement agencies throughout the country and abroad. Dayle specializes in Psychometry, the art of holding on to objects to see into the past, present and future. Through all these gifts she has been able to solve numerous murder cases, as well as finding missing children. Her special gift is helping people on a one-to-one basis.

While relaxing, Dayle and Blythe enjoy travel and playing with their German shepherds, as well as boating and golfing in Lake Tahoe and around the Hawaiian Islands.

If you want to address the author, write to Dayle Schear, P.O. Box 172, Zephyr Cove, NV 89448, or call (775) 588-3337. A phone reading with Dayle is $50 per session for about fifteen minutes. Please call (775) 588-3337 or in Hawaii call (808) 945-1188. Please let us know how you like this book *"Believe."*

Other Books/Tapes/Video
By Dayle Schear

Dare To Be Different (Autobiography) $16.00
The Psychic Within (True Psychic Stories) $14.95
Tarot For Beginners (Book) $ 6.95
Tarot For Beginners (Video) $24.95
Tarot For Beginners (Book & Video) $29.95

12-Meditation Tape Series (or $10 per) $59.95

Shipping Per Item $ 3.50

Please write me and let me know how this book has changed your life.

Write to: Dayle Schear
                  P. O. Box 172
                  Zephyr Cove, Nevada 89448
                  Phone (775) 588-5108
                  Web site: virtualworldpsychic.com
                  Email: ESP555555@aol.com